WORLD HOUSE NOW

contemporary architectural directions

First published in the United Kingdom in 2003
by Thames & Hudson Ltd,
181A High Holborn, London WC1V 7QX

www.thamesandhudson.com

© 2003 Universe Publishing
© 2003 Dung Ngo

British Library Cataloguing-in-Publication Data
A catalogue record for this book is available
from the British Library

ISBN 0-500-28419-9

Printed and bound in Italy

WORLD HOUSE NOW

contemporary architectural directions

Dung Ngo

Thames & Hudson

CONTENTS

✛ INTRODUCTION
Dung Ngo

In the twenty-first century the house physically and psychologically remains our place of shelter and sanctuary. The modern house continues to be the site of choice for formal experimentation, but it is also a finely calibrated indicator of a society's mindset. Perhaps more than any other building type, the house illustrates our preoccupation with technology, environment, global culture, and identity; in other words, with our ongoing engagement with modern life. Compiled in this volume are twenty nine houses from around the world that demonstrate the triumph of "regional modernism," where the influence of the international style is visible alongside the regional inflections of local building traditions and cultural preferences.

The effects of a global monoculture in the past few decades have threatened the survival of our local traditions and cultures, and our struggle against this loss have led to a search for the authentic in all forms of expression. This quest has resulted in the reexamination and revitalization of techniques and traditions that were abandoned in the embrace of technology and gadgetry. It's part of an alternative modernism visible in the sensuous and culturally-rooted work of the Mexican Luis Barragán or the topographically-driven buildings of the Portuguese Alvaro Siza. Some of the characteristics that characterize this alternative tradition are the fusing of new technologies with older building techniques, respect for the natural landscape, and sustainability. Without abandoning modernist concerns for function, economy, and formal innovation, this architecture embraces universal ideals and regional differences, embodying both globalism and localism, and produces houses that are rich in meaning, beautiful, as well as socially responsible. In other words, an architecture that represents the past *and* future of modernism.

LANDSCAPE

Many of the projects in this volume fully engage their surroundings, establishing a reciprocal relationship with the landscapes that give rise to them. Instead of flattening or razing the landscape for their construction, these houses cultivate their sites by allowing existing conditions to inform the house's form and construction. For instance, given an impossibly steep site on the outskirts of São

Paulo, the Brazilian architect Marcos Acayaba came up with an ingenious timber structural system that allows the Olga House (p. 12) to cantilever off its site with minimal impact on the land due to the use of columnar footings as its foundation. Respect for the natural landscape, a central tenet for this architecture, manifests in other ways. At the Dayton House (p. 132) in Minneapolis, architect Vincent James worked closely with the landscape architect George Hargreaves, gently molding the existing contours of the site to let the house merge with its surroundings. In Denton Corker Marshall's Sheep Ranch House (p. 86), in rural Victoria, Australia, the sweeping horizontality of the landscape is modulated by a series of concrete walls that mark and define the cluster of farming buildings. and at the same time add scale and measure to the spectacular setting.

Other examples in the bring the landscape into the very construction of the houses, further blurring the line between architecture and landscape, as in Samira Rathod's Karjat Farm House (p. 200) outside of Bombay, India; Kazuhiko Namba's Eco-Aluminum House (p. 176) in Tsukuba, Japan; and Claus Hermansen's Dyngby House (p. 116) in suburban Jylland, Denmark. In the case of the Karjat House, the design and construction of the house is wrapped around mature trees on the site, making them the focal points of the project. The Eco-Aluminum House (a prototype for pre-fabricated housing) acknowledges the "sitelessness" and high-tech nature of the project with a tree in the courtyard—so the house, literally, takes root. The Dyngby House also relies on nature, through the seasonal vines that cover the house's exterior, to continuously redefine the look of the house with the passing seasons. The South African architects van der Merwe Miszewski take this strategy one step further by using the umbrella pines that surround their Tree House (p. 212), in Cape Town, as visual and structural inspiration for the house's supporting columns.

LOCAL TRADITIONS

By using local materials and adapting constructional traditions, architects find another means to tie architecture to a specific locale. Rammed earth, a construction technique in which compacted soil constitutes the main building element, is used in Atelier Feichang Jianzhu's Split House (p. 62), near Beijing. This material choice is motivated by the architects' desire not only to take advantage of rammed earth's natural thermal insulating properties, but also to acknowledge the presence of another, more well-known structure nearby: the Great Wall. Rammed earth also appears in the Finnish architects Heikkinen/Komonen's Villa Eila (p. 110), located in the town of Mali, Guinea, where the local tradition of rammed earth construction was revitalized and applied to the geometric language of modernism. The result is a house that is both abstract and earthbound. In Adria Broid Rojkind's F-2 House (p. 20) volcanic basalt, a common local material in Mexico City, is used as visual and tactile contrast to the more pliant cast-in-place concrete. Conversely, corrugated metal found in the vernacular buildings of rural Australia is transformed in Glenn Murcutt's Kangaroo Valley House (p. 168), in New South Wales, to express the elegance of modernism's constructional precision. Regional construction techniques and traditional forms are also being reexamined by today's architects to inform and enrich modern houses. In the Studio House (p. 220) in Beijing, Ai Wei Wei uses a locally produced gray brick as well as ancient building traditions practiced by local builders to realize a resolutely modern, minimalist structure. The Korean-American architect Kyu Sung Woo's Stone Cloud House (p. 228) in Seoul, relies on the transformation of the ancient courtyard house layout as an expression of contemporary Korean culture.

Where possible, universal technological accoutrements, such as central air systems, have been abandoned in order to take advantage of local climate and more ecological means of ventilation. As demonstrated in the American firm LOOM Studio's Unfolding House (p. 160) in Bangkok, modern forms have been pressed into the service of time-proven strategies of air circulation and ventilation in a tropical climate, obviating the need for mechanized air conditioning. In Anupama Kundoo's Wall House (p. 154) in Auroville, India, a thick wall is oriented in such a way that it provides organizational logic for the building while also screening and absorbing the hot afternoon sun. Moveable partitions at James's Dayton House, Murcutt's Kangaroo Valley House, and Mathias Klotz's House 75 (p. 140) in Cantagua, Chile, allow sunlight and fresh air to be easily adjusted and controlled without mechanical methods.

TECHNOLOGY

Despite favoring the timeless over the timely, however, architects have not abandoned technology. On the contrary, in many cases, these architects push technology–whether in systems, construction, or material–to the limits to enhance or accentuate local conditions. The floating pool of Patkau Architects' Vancouver House (p. 192), for instance, which connects the house with the expansive bay beyond, would not be possible without constructional pyrotechnics. Seth Stein ingeniously employs an industrial carlift to transform the tiny Cheval Place (p. 206) in London into a showcase for vintage automobiles. Shigeru Ban's Naked House (p. 70) in Saitama, Japan, although inspired by the formal qualities of the agricultural sheds and greenhouses nearby, relies on the experimental use of artificial fruit-packing material as infill and insulation. The use of technologically advanced materials also enhances the sensual experience of the architecture itself. The Cor-ten steel cladding in ARO's Colorado House (p. 54), in Telluride, was spurred by the need for a durable exterior, but the metal's warm, oxidized-red texture provides a dramatic contrast to the field of aspen surrounding the house. Polycarbonate panels–a material more often used in industrial design–were employed in Andrade Morettin's D'Alessandro House (p. 38), outside São Paulo, to provide tantalizing, semi-transparent views into the home of a pair of photographers.

A number of houses included in this book are experiments, testing new construction methods and materials, but in all cases the projects rely on local expertise for their realization. Kruunenberg van der Erve's Laminata House (p. 146)–a high-tech structure built almost entirely of glass in Leerdam, the Netherlands–was sponsored and built by the local glass industry to challenge the limits of glass technology. Namba's Eco-Aluminum House explores the potential of a metal seldom used in residential construction, but in a form generated by the tradition of the Japanese courtyard house. Marcos Acayaba's collaborator in the Olga House was the client himself, Helio Olga, a structural engineer and builder who co-designed and fabricated the timber frame of the house.

ECOLOGY

Environmentalism, the call for social and ethical responsibility in our relationship to the land, is one of the driving themes for the architectural strategies discussed above, and most of the houses presented are informed by environmental concerns. As architects attempt to minimize or halt the destruction of the natural landscape, they've adopted alternative approaches to modern architecture: landscaping strategies that merge the houses with their sites; revitalizing older building techniques; and experimenting with new technologies and alternative. This key precept of sustainability is best demonstrated by the work of the Australian architect Glenn Murcutt, and his Kangaroo Valley House is a prime example. The architect's lifelong search for an architecture that embodies the identity of its users—and its builders—has resulted in a body of work that has gained the respect architects worldwide, and has strongly influenced many houses in this book. Using materials common in the local, vernacular buildings, such as corrugated metal and slender timber members, he produces houses that are environmentally aware and structurally non-invasive, an attitude that he describes as "touching the earth lightly." For Murcutt, architecture is about solutions and refinement, not innovations. Yet, in his search for the appropriate solution for a particular house and refinement of an architectural language, he nonetheless produces innovations. Murcutt arrives at final designs that are environmentally sound, site specific, and materially and constructionally appropriate, not through a willful imposition of prior beliefs, but by investigating and understanding the site, its culture, and its inhabitants. Physically one of the smallest house included in this survey, Murcutt's Kangaroo Valley House is also one of the most influential.

Brazil is a study in contrasts, and nowhere is this more apparent than in the city of São Paulo. South America's largest metropolis, São Paulo has over 25 million inhabitants. With a thriving population due to rural migration in recent decades, the city has swelled beyond the confines of its valley basin origins to build up the steep hills and mountainside that surround it. On this uneven and almost unbuildable terrain, the architect Marco Acayaba found inspiration for a prototype house designed for a progressive engineer/builder.

At the Olga House, Acayaba incorporates prefabricated elements into an environmentally sensitive design. On a vertiginous site, six concrete columns are sunk into the sloping ground, providing the support base for a standardized wood structure that frames the house. Above, four living levels are delineated by modular timber framing. Imbedded into the leveled hilltop is an open courtyard with a swimming pool, reminiscent of the California Case Study Houses of the 1950s and 1960s, especially Pierre Koenig's iconic Stahl House. The interior of the top floor is an uninterrupted, combined living/dining space, with an expansive view of the city skyline below in the distant horizon. The service core—the small galley kitchen, bathroom, and stairs—are grouped along the right side of the main living space, with the switchback stairs located at the center of the room to access the three levels underneath. The five bays of the top floor are reduced to three bays in the floor below which accommodates the bedrooms and bathrooms of the house, while the two single-bay floors beneath contain a guest room and an informal "play room" for the children.

Much of the house was fabricated off-site, and the whole assembly was completed by three workers in forty-five days. The modular, 10-foot by 10-foot timber bays are reinforced with diagonal steel bracing and infilled with a combination of glass and wood slats to screen the bright tropical sun. The resulting structure is a modern, inverted ziggurat that floats above its sloping terrain; not of the landscape yet respectful of it.

SÃO PAULO, BRAZIL **OLGA HOUSE** ✚

Marcos Acayaba Arquitetos

"With this system waste of material is reduced to a minimum," Acayaba commented, "with the final cost being half that of normal solutions for this kind of site." Acayaba has successfully refuted the perception that industrialized, prefabricated systems are not capable of producing beauty and are not destructive to the natural environment. In fact, he has designed other houses using the same construction technique, including his own house. Both the Olga House and Acayaba's own house have won major architectural prizes in Brazil, proving that his novel building techniques are recognized as an alternative to the conventional practice.

RIGHT ✚ The inverted ziggurat form of the Olga House, resting on concrete pillars, floats above its steeply sloping site.
OVERLEAF ✚ The house is entered from the top floor, which is connected to the access road by an open courtyard containing a swimming pool.

15

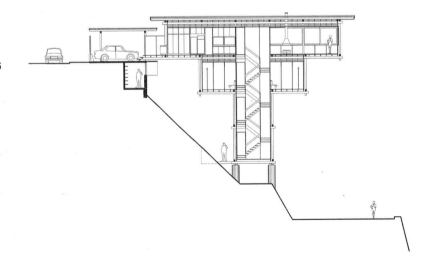

ABOVE + Six concrete pillars in two parallel rows support the modular timber frame above; the structure is further stabilized by connecting the top level to a retaining wall embedded into the courtyard. **RIGHT** + Pre-cast concrete panels are assembled to form the floors and ceilings of the house, which are covered in tiles and wood.

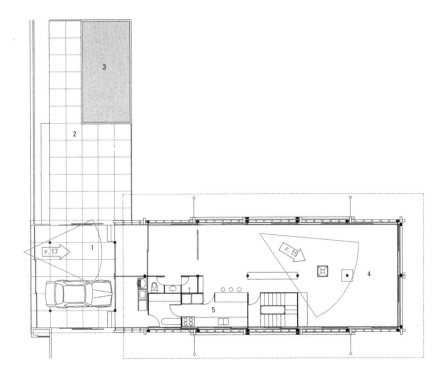

MAIN FLOOR

1 garage
2 terrace
3 pool
4 living / dining
5 kitchen

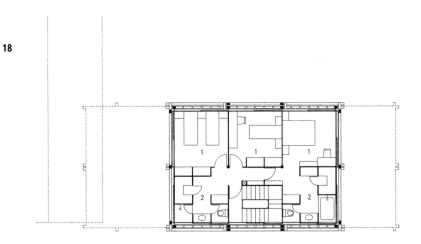

BEDROOM FLOOR

1 bedroom
2 bathroom

RIGHT + The expansive living space, with built-in bookshelves and seating, provides a spectacular view of downtown São Paulo.

Mexico City is the indisputable cultural and political capital of Latin America. From the Corbusier-inspired house and studio by Juan O'Gorman designed for Diego Rivera and Frida Kahlo to Luis Barragán's regionally-inflected structures of color and light, Mexico City has always provided fertile ground for modernist architecture.

The F-2 House, by the architects Miquel Adriá, Isaac Broid, and Michel Rojkind, is an elegant and spatially complex design. Built in one of Mexico City's new affluent neighborhoods, the house is discreetly sited behind walls constructed from volcanic basalt. Drawing on an old tradition of building with the volcanic stone widely available in the region, the basalt walls are incorporated into the dynamic, interlocking volumes of the house itself. Like Mies van der Rohe's floating planes of onyx at the Barcelona Pavilion, these stone walls are not deployed structurally, but are placed to define spatial volumes and frame views on the site.

The house is laid out in an L-shape configuration, with the longer arm running parallel to the entry path. The sloping site is revealed in the entry sequence, where an angled basalt wall along the house leads to the expansion of the second arm: a three-story, cast-concrete volume resting on thin columnar *pilotis*, making references to both Mies and Le Corbusier. The large interior comprises few enclosed rooms, the designers opting instead for a strategy of overlapping volumes. Light-flooded spaces are interspersed with shadowy areas, enhancing the play of natural light in the house.

The entry floor, the house's middle level, is a series of rooms—bath, kitchen, dining—placed sequentially, terminating with the large living space around the bend of the L-plan. The top floor is divided into three bedrooms and their bathrooms, although here, too, openings in the concrete walls tie these spaces, visually and volumetrically, back to the main space through a dramatic, top-lit stairway that connects all the levels along the back of the house. The bottom floor, built into the sloping site, houses a family space, which opens out to the flat grassy yard beyond.

✚ **F-2 HOUSE** MEXICO CITY, MEXICO
Adriá Broid Rojkind Arquitectos

The architectural language employed at the F-2 House is modern, but the use of materials and light is proudly regional. The play of light raking across the indigenous basalt and board-formed cast concrete reveals a character and sensibility that is purely Mexican in spirit.

LEFT ✚ The triple-story wing of the F-2 House is an interplay of positive and negative volumes, achieved with the use of board-formed cast concrete and glass. The three levels house the master bedroom suite at the top, the living room at the middle, and the family game room at the bottom.

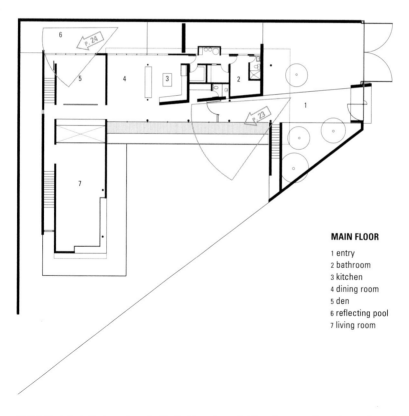

MAIN FLOOR

1 entry
2 bathroom
3 kitchen
4 dining room
5 den
6 reflecting pool
7 living room

TOP + The entry to the house is marked by flanking columns holding afloat a cantilevered travertine roof. **RIGHT +** The main volume of the house is revealed with the entry sequence, which is defined by a teak and basalt gravel pathway.

LEFT ✦ View of the den through the openings in the cast concrete wall; the reflecting pond is filled with the same basalt rocks used in the surrounding exterior walls. **ABOVE ✦** The concrete staircase connecting the three levels of the house ending at the master bedroom on the third floor. **OVERLEAF ✦** The living room's thick concrete walls impart a sculptural quality to the space.

For over twenty-five years, Tadao Ando has consistently produced a singular architecture in his signature material of cast concrete. Ando is a self-taught designer, and his structures reveal influences from the early masters of Modernism but also from his days as a Japanese master carpenter's apprentice.

Although concrete is not considered a traditional Japanese building material, in Ando's hands it is treated with the same reverence and care as the precious woods used in temples and houses. Indeed, for most of his career Ando was known for his houses and churches, hauntingly spare spaces built mostly in and around Osaka, where he maintains his practice. Ando has slowly started building outside of Japan, to meet overwhelming international demands. "This is my first building in the United States," Ando stated about the Chicago House, "and the fact that the site is in a city that possesses many well-known works of architecture made the commission especially exciting."

Located in the leafy neighborhood of Lincoln Park, the Chicago House is built on one side of a wide lot; the other side is left open, creating an outdoor space that is an integral part of the house. The house is composed of three distinct parts: a two-story volume at the front containing the entry and guest rooms; a three-story volume in the back containing the private living quarters and master bedroom suite. Connecting the two volumes is a long but spacious, combined living/dining room. Above this single-story living space is a large terrace, enclosed by a concrete wall on one side and glass partitions on the other. It forms a meditative space that is the heart of the house's activities during the warm months. A large, gently sloped ramp connects the two levels, functioning not only as circulation but also as a viewing platform for the reflecting pool that nearly covers the open half of the site.

✚ CHICAGO HOUSE CHICAGO, ILLINOIS
Tadao Ando Architect

Spaces are delineated by a series of parallel concrete walls that gradually unfold from the more private and enclosed side of the house to the openness of the tranquil courtyard. Unlike Frank Lloyd Wright's Prairie houses nearby, Ando's house is inwardly focused. In this respect, the Chicago House has more in common with Chicago's other famous architect, Mies van der Rohe–specifically, Mies's unbuilt courtyard house designs.

The tranquility achieved in the Chicago House is typical of Ando's work. The theme of sanctuary is always present in his houses, and in this sense, Ando has successfully transplanted the spirit of his native Osaka to a kindred but foreign city.

RIGHT ✚ A series of parallel concrete walls define and reveal the enclosed spaces of the Chicago House, culminating with the free-standing structures that frame the edge of the reflecting pool.

LEFT ✛ The focal point of the house is a second story terrace that overlooks the reflecting pool. The living room beneath the terrace also connects the major volumes of the house at the two ends of the site. **ABOVE, OVERLEAF** ✛ The outdoor terrace is reached by a ramp from the living space on the ground floor.

FIRST FLOOR

1 entry court
2 entry hall
3 guest room
4 living / dining
5 reflecting pool
6 kitchen
7 sitting room
8 library
9 bedroom
10 garden
11 garage

SECOND FLOOR

1 guest room
2 terrace
3 ramp
4 bedroom

RIGHT ✛ The ramp, a visually dynamic feature in this otherwise serene structure, can be viewed from almost every room in the house. **OVERLEAF ✛** The reflecting pool as viewed from the living room, which contains the single free-standing column in the cast-in-place concrete structure.

New materials are frequently used in modern construction, but they are often exploited for their structural characteristics rather than for their poetic qualities. At the D'Alessandro House, new materials are mixed with old to heighten and transform daily living experiences.

Located on a densely wooded lot on the outskirts of São Paulo, this small house was sited to avoid the removal of any of the mature trees on the site. The house's two simple volumes are arranged parallel to each other and connected by two openings. The larger of the two volumes is an open space framed by a wooden structure and enclosed with polycarbonate panels. The slightly refractive quality of this plastic material both reveals and hides the interior of the house when seen from the outside, while the whole interior is bathed in natural light. This light-filled single room contains the living space and the sleeping area, which can be temporarily enclosed by a retractable curtain. One corner of the volume is clad with transparent glass, allowing unobstructed views of the verdant surrounding and a small pond beyond the property line. A thin roof composed of metal thermo-acoustical tiles is detached and seems to hover above the house, further emphasizing the lightness of the structure.

Andrade Morettin Arquitetos Associados
✛ D'ALLESANDRO HOUSE SÃO PAULO, BRAZIL

The companion volume to the living space is a solid service core, consciously designed as a counterpoint to the open pavilion. Constructed from solid brick walls, the service volume houses the kitchen, bathroom, laundry facilities, and water and gas reservoirs. Its also shields the living space from the harsh western sun.

Designed for a photographer couple, the D'Alessandro House functions as a living camera by day, taking in the ever-changing views afforded by the shifting play of light and shadows created by the surrounding trees, while at night the house becomes a light box, reflecting back into the landscape the life inside.

LEFT ✛ The translucent living pavilion floats above its concrete foundation, while a solid service core nestles to one side.
OVERLEAF ✛ The small house is sited in a clearing on the heavily wooded lot. Glimpses of the interior can be viewed through the semi-transparent polycarbonate panels that sheath the living space.

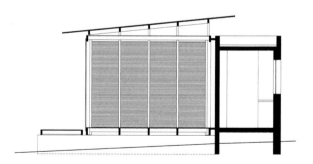

SECTION

ABOVE, RIGHT ✛ One corner of the living pavilion is glazed in clear glass to provide an unobstructed view to the exterior.
OVERLEAF ✛ Light and privacy in the sleeping area can be modulated with a curtain hung from tracks in the ceiling.

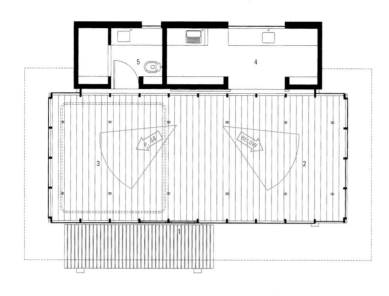

PLAN

1 deck entry
2 living
3 sleeping
4 kitchen
5 bathroom

Classical architecture often employs symmetry to convey purity and grandeur. Modernism, on the other hand, with its emphasis on dynamic movement and formal tension, tends toward asymmetry. Yet more often than not, modern architecture relies on symmetry to play up its kinetic formal expression. Le Corbusier's early work, which was highly influenced by the underlining geometry of Palladio's classical architecture, brilliantly used symmetry as the counterpoint to his dynamic plans and elevations. The Clifford House, by the architecture firm Architectus, takes this interplay between symmetry and asymmetry one step further, introducing a rigorously ordered structure to a highly irregular site.

Located in one of Auckland's more hilly suburbs, the site is a sloping triangular plot that terminates with a tidal basin. An abundance of mature trees and neighboring houses nearby were additional siting constraints for the architects. In plan, the house employs an east-west bilateral symmetry, with a Palladian nine-square grid detectable in the division of functional program on each floor. Plans can be deceiving, however, especially when topography, movement, and details are taken in account.

An angled set of steps descends along the slope of the site to the house's entry court which also acts as an outdoor terrace. Entering the interior of this main floor on axis, the visitor's geometric balance is subtly subverted with the placement of the kitchen on the immediate right and the staircase on the left. Further into the space the visual direction turns ninety degrees in the large living/dining area, whose cantilevered outdoor decks punctuate the north-south axis.

While these deviations from the symmetry of the plan are dictated by functional requirements and the irregularity of the land, they also soften and enliven the plan's rigid geometry. Below this main floor is a bedroom/bathroom suite reserved for guests, while the upstairs houses a bathroom and two bedrooms separated by a dressing area.

Except for two angled concrete-block walls, which provide visual privacy from the approaching road and block the western sun, the house's structure consists of thin, laminated timber posts and vast expanses of glass infilling. Wooden shutters are used where sunlight needs to be controlled, while the use of semi-opaque glass provides visual contrast to the transparency of the house. Simply detailed, joineries between the wood, steel, and glass members place the visual emphasis not on ornament but on the overall quality of the spaces themselves.

By juxtaposing the rigorous but serene geometry of the house with its unique site, the architects have created a viewing stage for the spectacular scenery outside the house, and the contemplative daily activities within.

47

LEFT + The transparency of the Clifford House belies its suburban site. Privacy is achieved by siting of the house, taking advantage of the uneven topography and the mature plantings on the lot.

THIRD FLOOR

1 bathroom
2 bedroom
3 dressing room

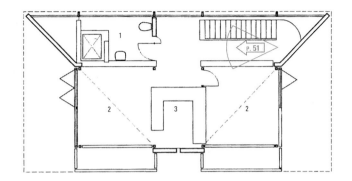

SECOND FLOOR

1 terrace
2 entry
3 kitchen
4 dining
5 living
6 deck

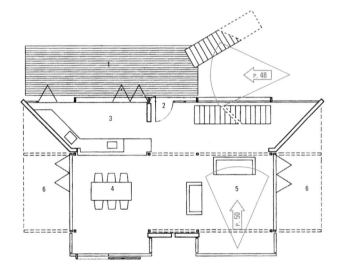

LEFT + Steps take the visitor from the access road into the entry terrace, secluded visually from both the road and neighboring houses.

LEFT ✛ The exposed ceiling joists are echoed in the open-grilled balustrade of the staircase. **ABOVE** ✛ The bedrooms and bathroom are located on the third floor. A clerestory of adjustable glass louvers allow natural air to circulate. **OVERLEAF** ✛ The open living/dining space is defined on one side by the service zone containing the kitchen and staircase, bracketed to the north and south by wood decks.

53

In the foothills of the Colorado Rockies, where rolling green hills of aspen trees are interrupted only by spectacular mountain peaks, Stephen Cassell and Adam Yarinski of Architecture Research Office (ARO) have built a house that lives up to its majestic settings.

Set on a knoll at the edge of a large aspen meadow, the Colorado House is composed of a series of parallel planes–concrete retaining walls embedded in the hill. Although these walls are structural, they also serve as the organizing elements of the house. The architects have devised a plan in which the placement of the parallel walls softens and modulates their unrelenting geometry as they descend the hillside, with interior, exterior, as well as circulation spaces slipped in between the walls. The plan is surprisingly flexible, able to generate living spaces of all sizes. The walls vary not only in length, but also in height and in relation to one another; the plan also modulates spaces within the house vertically, with double-height rooms anchoring one end of the house.

On the exterior, the concrete walls are wrapped in Cor-ten steel–a pre-oxidized weathering metal that, when it rusts, turns a warm, reddish-brown color. The top layer of oxidation protects the metal underneath, making it the ideal cladding material for extreme weather. At certain points along the walls, the Cor-ten steel moves from the outside to the inside, accentuating the relationship of exterior spaces and interior rooms.

Inside, large open spaces are staggered from one another to reinforce the slipping notion of the parallel walls. Entry is set discreetly between two close walls, which open up to reveal the kitchen and dining room, considered by the architects as the central social focus of the house. An opening to the right of the kitchen leads to a large living room, which reveals itself as a mezzanine to the dramatic double-height space at one end. Bedrooms and bathrooms are more modest spaces on the periphery of the plan.

+ COLORADO HOUSE TELLURIDE, COLORADO
Architecture Research Office

All of this–the placement of walls, the modulation of ceiling heights, the distribution of spaces–is done to create vistas of the sweeping landscape beyond. In framing views of the natural surroundings and giving it a sense of measure through the architecture, ARO has managed not only to capture the experience of living at the foot of the Rockies, but to enhance it.

RIGHT + The interlocking volumes of the Colorado House rise above the meadow, framing the scenic views beyond.

ABOVE + The rigorous plan composed of parallel walls is only evident from the side. **RIGHT +** The placement of the concrete retaining walls follow the contours of the sloping site, creating a variety of interior and exterior spaces.

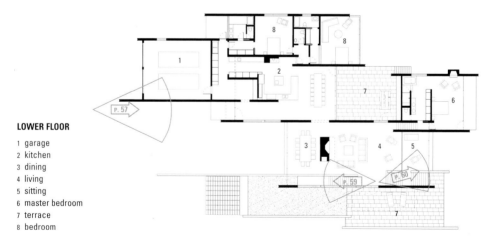

LOWER FLOOR

1 garage
2 kitchen
3 dining
4 living
5 sitting
6 master bedroom
7 terrace
8 bedroom

ABOVE + The retaining walls are clad in Cor-ten steel—a pre-oxidized weathering metal that, when it rusts, turns a warm, reddish-brown color. **LEFT +** Stairs inserted between structural walls lead to a partial lower level (not shown in plan above). **OVERLEAF +** The sitting room's glass end wall presents a spectacular view of an aspen meadow and the Rocky Mountains.

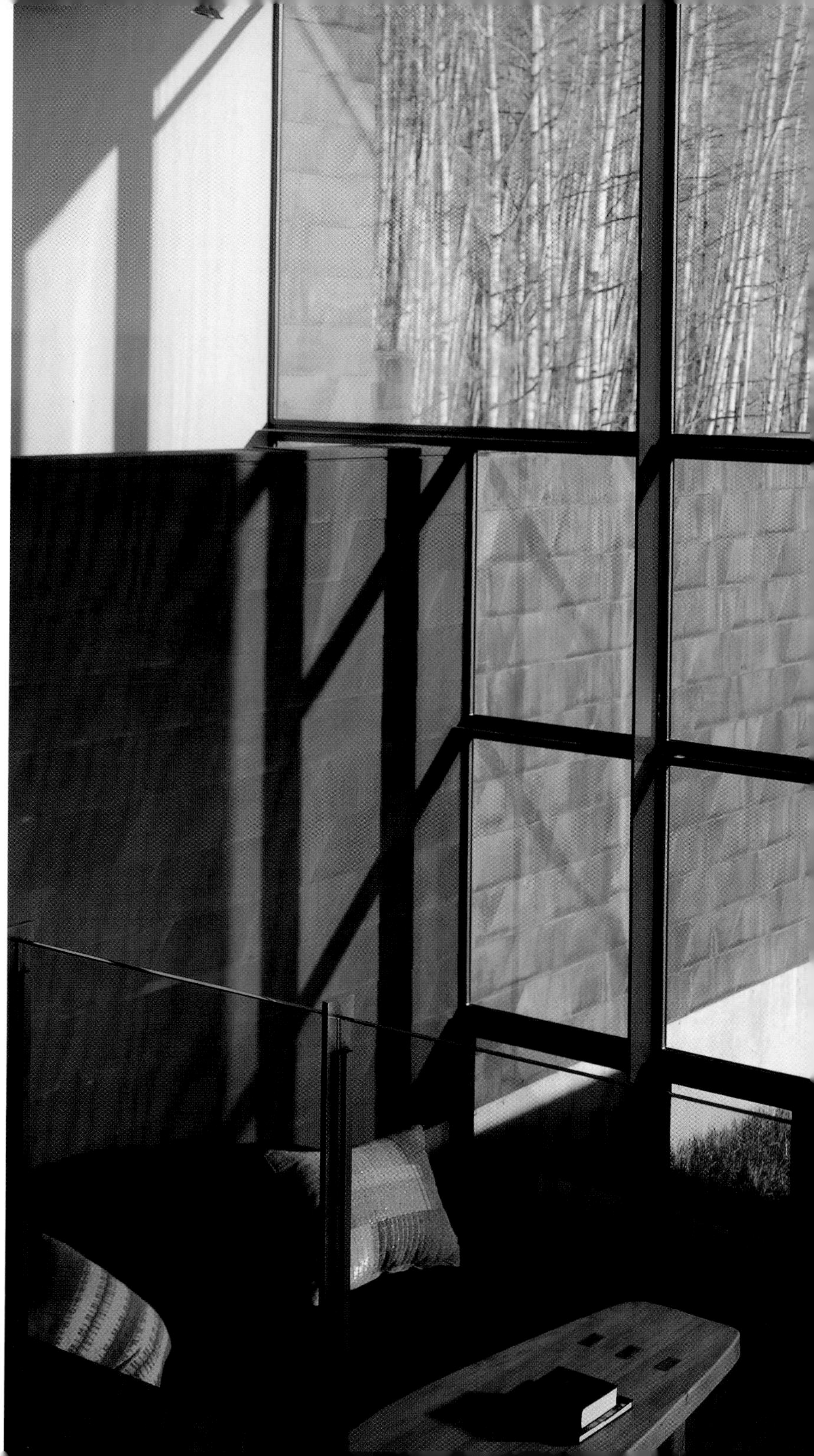

The Chinese concept of Shan Shui literally means "mountain/water." It refers to the state of balance and harmony prized so highly in the classical Chinese arts. While Shan Shui is traditionally applied in Chinese landscape painting, it is equally relevant to building and landscape construction. Feng Shui—the art of proper arrangement now so popular in the West—is actually a specific *practice* of Shan Shui. Both the concept of Shan Shui and the practice of Feng Shui are abstract principles of balance and counterbalance, meant to take on specific manifestations as they are applied to specific conditions. Rather than prescribing inflexible rules or aesthetics, the idea of Shan Shui encourages harmony, whether it is spiritual, technological, or ecological.

BEIJING, CHINA **SPLIT HOUSE** ✛

Atelier Feichang Jianzhu

The Split House, located in a semi-rural area north of Beijing, opens conceptually and literally to receive the mountain and water, and the precepts of Shan Shui. The basic scheme of the Split House is two bars that together form the structure, with the third element—the courtyard in between—completing the composition. The courtyard house is a time-honored type in Chinese architecture, one that takes advantage of both built and natural landscapes by blurring their boundaries. The angle between the two halves of the Split House–designed as prototype–can be adjusted to fit on almost any given site. The two bars can be placed in parallel, at right angles, or any position in between to conform to the particular landscape.

The main walls of the Split House are made of load-bearing rammed earth–an indigenous construction technique used to build the nearby Great Wall. By using local material available on the site—excavated soil from the leveled courtyard—the construction minimizes the environmental impact and also pays respect to the grandeur of the surrounding landscape.

One enters the house through a glass vestibule pavilion which connects its two halves. A creek–the "water" of Shan Shui–running down the middle of the house can be seen through the glass floor. Functionally, the house is also split evenly in half, living spaces in one wing and kitchen and dining room in the other. The second level of both wings contains bedroom suites, whose open decks on each end further connect the outdoors with the indoor spaces.

Yung-Ho Chang, Atelier Feichang Jianzhu's principal, notes that "China is presently undergoing a great transitional period. The opportunity for architects goes beyond building to the shaping of contemporary Chinese society itself." In the Split House, Chang has incorporated Western techniques and aesthetics to reshape China's unique building culture without losing sight of local identity and traditions.

RIGHT ✛ The entrance of the Split House is a glass vestibule located at the point where the structure "splits."
OVERLEAF ✛ A terraced courtyard is created by the two wings of the house, drawing the landscape into the interior.

SECOND FLOOR

1 bedroom
2 bathroom
3 sitting room
4 roof terrace

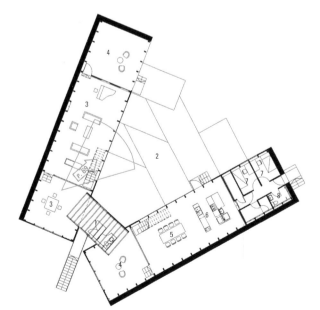

FIRST FLOOR

1 entry pavilion
2 courtyard
3 living room
4 covered porch
5 dining room
6 kitchen
7 bedroom
8 bathroom

ABOVE + Roof decks at either ends of the wings of the house are accessed from the bedrooms and provide a more intimate out-door space than the shared courtyard.

ABOVE ✛ The creek running across the site is visible through the vestibule pavilion's glass floor. **RIGHT** ✛ Sculptural wood and steel stairs highlight the open interior of the living spaces .

Flexible space is the ultimate modernist dream: the ability to reconfigure a space to accommodate varying uses, moods and spatial relationships. The quest for flexibility spawned the open plan–the abandonment of fixed walls in favor of free-flowing spaces. In the Naked House, the Japanese architect Shigeru Ban takes this idea one step further by unanchoring the rooms themselves, so that they can roam freely.

Ban challenges preconceptions of how houses are lived in. His series of "Case Study" houses–consciously modeled after the famous California houses of the 1950s and 60s–explores the freedom of the open plan by banishing all fixed walls, as in the case in his Wall-less House, or by literally employing a "curtain wall," used to dramatic effect in his Curtain Wall House. In the Naked House, signature elements of his past projects are present, such as moving partitions and unrolling curtains, used to temporarily define interior and exterior spaces. But here, building on a flat site surrounded by rice fields, Ban turns the focus inward to explore the dynamic relationship between rooms within a larger space. Inspired by the greenhouse sheds that populate this agricultural area north of Tokyo, the Naked House is an elongated, double-height, single space enclosed by a translucent skin. Regular wood-stud construction with metal X-bracings is used to build the framing, infilled with sealed plastic bags that contain polyethylene strands, a material normally used to package fruit. Corrugated fiberglass sheeting covers the exterior, while translucent nylon fabric stretches over the wooden frame of the house's interior. The resulting 15-inch-thick walls are well-insulated but allow a beautiful, diffused light to enter through the longitudinal side walls. One end of the large rectangular space of the shed is enclosed with rolling glazed walls, while the other end houses the bathroom and communal dressing area. The kitchen is located along one side wall, which can be closed off with rolling white curtains.

KAWAGOE, JAPAN **NAKED HOUSE** +
Shigeru Ban Architects

Within this neutral white space, four cubic rooms–each one an individual living unit for a family member–roll about on wheels. Constructed from brown paper honeycomb panels on wooden frames, these boxes provide work and play space on top and sleeping areas inside. Untethered, the rooms move around for different configurations within the space. They can be temporarily anchored near a wall to hook up with wall-mounted air conditioners and heaters, or rolled out to the canopied terrace for sleeping under the stars. With the Naked House, Shigeru Ban has successfully employed the time-honored language of light construction and shoji walls to reflect the age of global mobility.

71

LEFT + Resembling a greenhouse shed, the Naked House is surrounded by rice paddies. **OVERLEAF** + The interior is one large, double-height space, with the service core of bathroom and kitchen located along the perimeter walls.

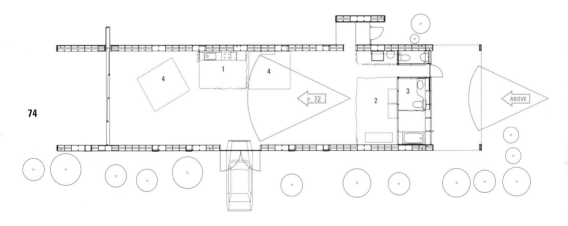

PLAN

1 kitchen
2 dressing room
3 bathroom
4 mobile rooms

ABOVE + a row of shutters allows light and air to enter the bathroom. **RIGHT +** The wood-frame structure is covered in corrugated fiberglass on the exterior, a plastic membrane on the interior, and is insulated by sealed polyethelyne fruit packing bags, custom-made by the architect's studio.

77

LEFT + The rolling boxes act as bedrooms with play spaces above. **ABOVE** + Curtains are used to enclose the kitchen and the communal dressing/bathing area.

The myth of the "primitive house" claims the ordinary dwelling as the origin of all architecture; architectural historians theorize that the first house was either a hut or a cave. Depending on interpretation, the cave provided fortification from inclement weather, while the hut was built in response to a gentle climate. But both hut and cave provided our ancestors with shelter, comfort, and security. Drawing on these sources, the Spanish architect Alberto Campo Baeza has designed an elegant modern house that recalls the origins of architecture.

Built on a rural site outside of Madrid, the de Blas House is deceptively simple, consisting of a glass and steel pavilion floating serenely on a concrete plinth. Although Spain's most well-known architects are usually associated with the exuberant sensibilities of the Catalán region—as exemplified by the architecture of Barcelona—Campo Baeza belongs to the more restrained school of Madrid architecture. His architecture is characterized by crisp geometry, unfussy details, and most of all, a sense of pure calm and serenity.

Built into the sloping site, the concrete walls gently nest into the hillside. "Above all else," Campo Baeza says, "the house is a response to its location." The structure is entered on the lower level, through a discreet door on the down side of the slope. The lower level houses most of the living spaces: a series of simple rooms placed sequentially, containing living, dining, bedrooms, bathrooms, and kitchen. One large window in the living room offers a view to the exterior, but otherwise the concrete walls are only occasionally punctured by small openings that allow light in but resolutely retain the sense of security and privacy of the "cave."

MADRID, SPAIN **DE BLAS HOUSE +**
Estudio Arquitectura Campo Baeza

By contrast, an open glass pavilion sits atop the concrete living-level plinth, accessible by the interior stairs alone. Composed of a delicately glazed steel structure painted white, the space functions as a viewing platform where the owner can contemplate the surrounding landscape and the mountain range beyond. A pool at this level also doubles as a reflecting, meditative surface. The glass pavilion is reminiscent of Mies van der Rohe's Farnsworth Pavilion, the archetypal modern house. Here, however, the pure space has no functional requirements except as a space of contemplation.

Although contemporary building technology allows us to ignore extreme weather, we still seek security in the "cave" and delight in the "hut." At Campo Baeza's de Blas House, the owner was given both.

RIGHT + The "hut" above and the "cave" are reinterpreted through the language of modernism with a glass pavilion floating serenely above a concrete plinth.

ABOVE ✚ The glass pavilion recalls the Farnsworth House by Mies van der Rohe, whose work greatly influenced Campo Baeza.
RIGHT ✚ The surrounding landscape is gradually revealed by ascending the stairs.

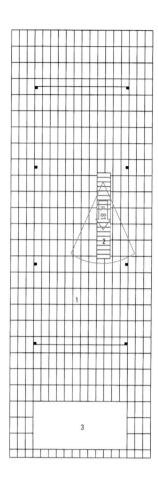

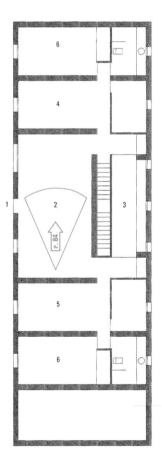

UPPER FLOOR

1 pavilion
2 stairs
3 reflecting pool

LOWER FLOOR

1 entry
2 living room
3 kitchen
4 dining room
5 study
6 bedroom

RIGHT ✛ The stairs connects the two levels and acts as the spine for the arrangement for the lower floor rooms.
OVERLEAF ✛ The slope of the site affords spectacular views to the outside from the relative security of the living quarters.

The first human settlements were farming communities, formed by people who achieved a certain level of mastery over nature by cultivating land and domesticating animals. The desire for permanence, however, goes beyond a steady control of food sources; the human need to mark the land is intimately tied to our understanding of community. The architectural organization strategy of the Sheep Ranch House takes its cue from this desire to make one's mark upon the land.

Denton Corker Marshall

VICTORIA, AUSTRALIA **SHEEP RANCH HOUSE** +

Located near a historic farming community in the territory of Victoria, the landscape surrounding the Sheep Ranch House is typical of Australia: spectacular rolling hills of grass under a bright sun and the large, blue dome sky. The architectural firm of Denton Marshall Corker responded to this overwhelming landscape with a modern sheep ranch. The farming homestead complex consists of a main house, a guest wing, and sheds for the sheep pens and machinery. Yet instead of grouping the discrete structures in a typical farm layout, the architects organized the

different parts with a series of imposing concrete walls, which cohere the assemblage of disparate buildings. This bold gesture establishes the farm's overall identity, and marks definitively its location within the vast landscape. Additionally, the walls take the place of the usual lines of trees planted in the region as windbreaks. Approached from afar, the walls appear as a series of abstract outcroppings, peeking out from the rolling hills. Upon arrival, an open courtyard is revealed, where the daily activities of a sheep farm take place. The main house is situated behind the darker, central concrete wall, which does not hint at the scale or domesticity. Passing through the opening, however, reveals the living quarters, along with the dramatic landscape beyond the glass partitions.

Both the main house and the guest wing resemble modern day lean-to sheds, with sloping roofs resting on the concrete walls. The enclosures of these lean-to structures, though, are translated into steel and glass, affording an uninterrupted view of most of the property, a practical consideration for a sheep farm that nonetheless provides a stunning backdrop for the living quarters. The rooms are organized rigorously but simply, always with the view of the landscape and the harsh weather taken into account. Although not always visible from within the house, the concrete walls continue to act as the measure between the manmade interiors and the limitless landscape beyond.

LEFT + The fully-glazed house is protected from the harsh sun by the deep overhang of the roof. **OVERLEAF** + The monumental concrete walls marking the Sheep Ranch House appear as abstract rocky outcrops.

PLAN

1 courtyard
2 garage
3 living / dining
4 bedroom
5 work yard
6 shearing shed

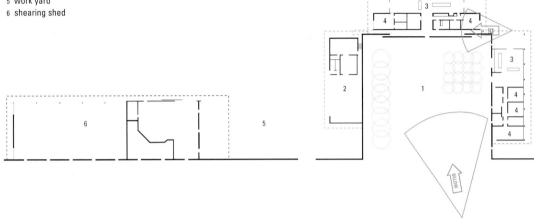

LEFT + A forecourt of gravel organizes the daily activities of the sheep ranching operation; the darker, central wall signifies the house's entry. **ABOVE +** Breezeways running between the concrete walls and the living quarters provide a respite from the strong sun. **OVERLEAF +** The simple modernist interior of the house reflects the utilitarian nature of the complex.

93

Istanbul has always been viewed culturally as a city at the crossroads. Located at the mouth of the Bosphorus Straits—which connects the Mediterranean Sea to the Black Sea—the city is a seamless blend of East and West, old and new. Its location is not just geographically and politically advantageous, Istanbul is also strategically located for stunning views. In order to preserve the natural beauty of the land overlooking the Bosphorus water edge, the city recently passed an ordinance forbidding new construction along the strait unless it follows the height and footprint of pre-existing buildings. The Flooded House deftly navigates these constraints, producing an architecture that embraces the new without abandoning the old.

The modest 19th-century structure built on the site was once intended as housing for priests; in the design of the new house Gokhan Avcioglu of GAD Architecture retains the historic feel of the original structure as well its dimensions. "Our greatest challenge was to make a modern living space within the footprint of the old house," Avcioglu explains. Original locations of doors and windows remain, and the exterior envelope is sheathed in the vernacular horizontal wooden boards. The pitched roof and the small balconies on the second and third floors echo the structure's previous history. The house is entered at the ground floor, which is now a single-space living room. Likewise, the upstairs interiors, stripped and restructured, now functions as a large master bedroom suite. One level

down from the ground floor is a partially buried space, still conforming to the house's original footprint, but opening out on one side to a large outdoor terrace with sweeping views of the Bosphorus and the city beyond. Here Avcioglu pulls off an ingenious architectural sleight-of-hand: the terrace is in fact the roof of a much larger floor below. While respecting the original envelope, the architect was able to introduce new living spaces beneath the old frame of the house. This sub-basement level houses the garage, gym, cellar, another living room, and—most spectacularly—an indoor pool. The open side of this bottom level opens out to an outdoor pool and the lawn beyond. By excavating and burying, the architect was able to double the square footage. Underground spaces always encounter the problem of light, which is solved here with three organically-shaped skylights, two over the indoor pool and gym and a third above the living room.

GAD Architecture

ISTANBUL, TURKEY **FLOODED HOUSE +**

95

The house is considered by the architect and owners as "flooded," referencing the two man-made pools as well as the Bosphorus immediately beyond, water being an inseparable part of Istanbul's identity. But one can also view the house, a modern structure built upon layers of memory, as flooded with living history.

LEFT + The four stories of the Flooded House occupy the footprint of original 19th century building, in accordance with local zoning laws.

97

LEFT ✛ Wooden battens and stone masonry bridge the traditional form of the house with its modern detailing.
ABOVE ✛ Curvilinear skylights illuminate the sub-basement living spaces.

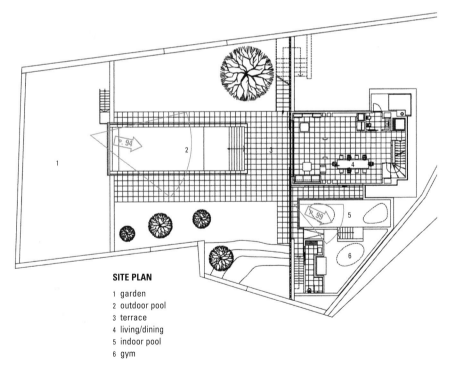

SITE PLAN

1 garden
2 outdoor pool
3 terrace
4 living/dining
5 indoor pool
6 gym

RIGHT + The indoor pool provides a visual and spiritual connection with the Bosphorus Strait near the ancient site.

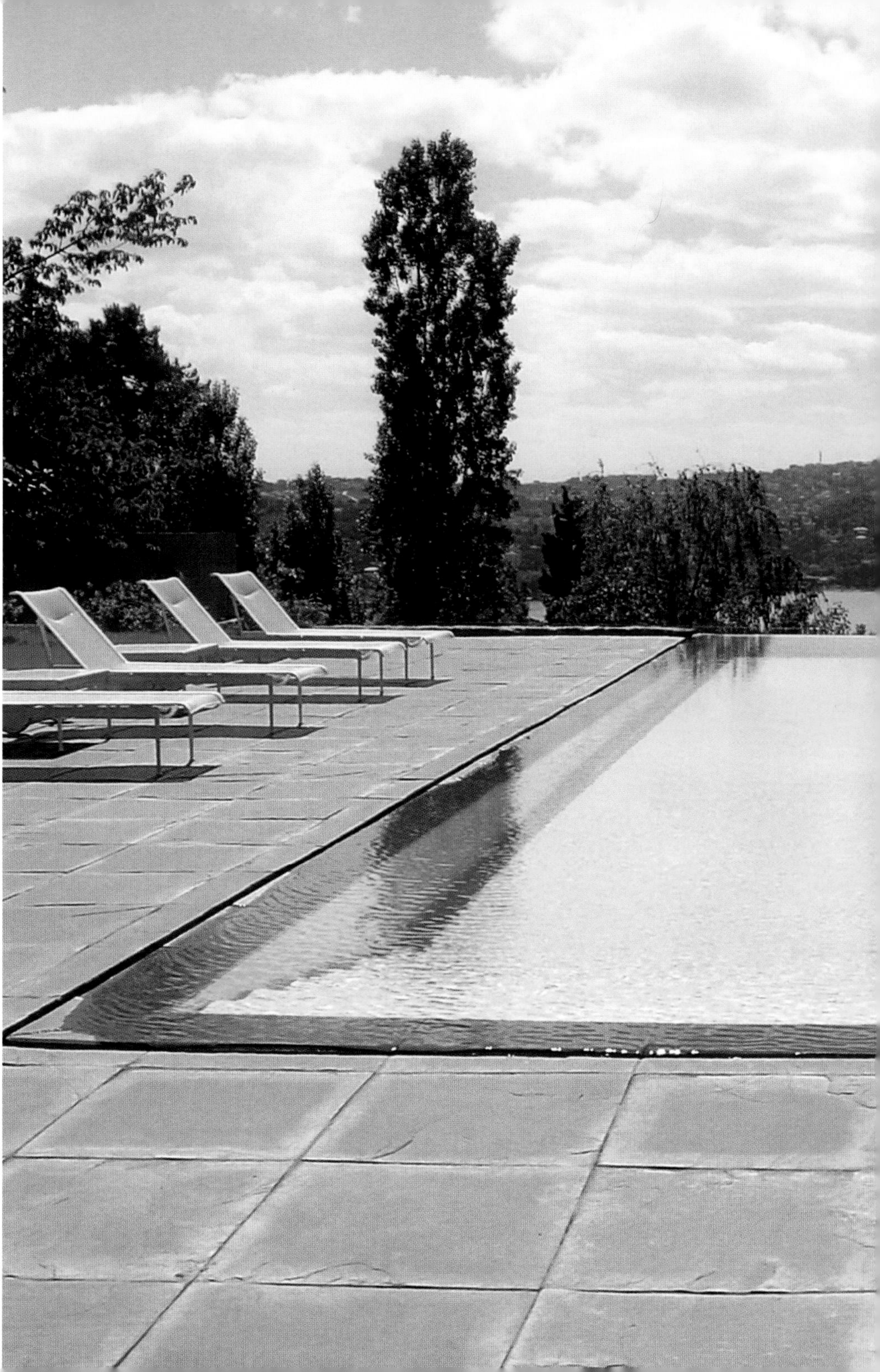

The exterior skin of a building can offer many clues to the nature of the spaces inside. This is especially true in houses. Through its skin, a house can sustain itself by bringing inside air and sunlight. Sean Godsell's Peninsula House, not unlike some of the plants that grow in the region, can close in on itself or open out–depending on the weather and particular desires of the owners. Indeed, the house features layered exterior walls that can modulate and adjust to the temperate climate and strong sunlight of Australia's coast, where the house is located.

Godsell embedded an oxidized steel structure on the side of a sand dune to form the skeleton of the house. Three sides, including the top, of this structure feature a skin of wooden shutters, thin panels of timber strips hung vertically to create a porous membrane. On the inside of the steel frame, Godsell attached glass panels, also operable. In combination, the two membranes can be adjusted, depending on the time of day or the season of the year, to permit varying degrees of openness. In effect, the two skins protect the house's interior from harsh light and inclement weather, but do not shut it out completely. Its inhabitants can, in effect, "tune" the house to the weather and the time of day through the sun's movement.

VICTORIA, AUSTRALIA **PENINSULA HOUSE** +
Sean Godsell Architect

A simple two-story structure is nested within this double skin, with rooms laid out simply and elegantly. Through an open-air carport, the entry at the top of the dune leads to stairs to the lower level. Here, a double-height space contains the house's living functions, with an entire glass wall at one end that can be opened to the veranda outside. The private living spaces are located on the upper level, with the bathroom opening out to a private courtyard.

Diaphanous yet protective, precise yet flexible, the exterior of the Peninsula House reveals the life of the interior without exposing it.

RIGHT + An outer skin of operable wooden shutters is hung off the oxidized steel structure of the Peninsula House, allowing light to penetrate its membrane.

LEFT + The large glass endwall of the house opens up on clear days to unobstructed views out to the waterfront.
ABOVE + The operable shutters also hinge upwards to allow for unimpeded circulation.

UPPER FLOOR

1 carport
2 storage
3 courtyard
4 bathroom
5 bedroom
6 open to below

P.96

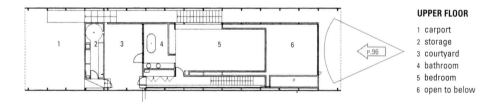

TOP + A wooden side deck is anchored by an outdoor fireplace for nights under the stars. **RIGHT +** Al fresco living continues with the master bathroom, which opens out to a private courtyard. **OVERLEAF +** The simple geometry of the house contrasts with its sophisticated cladding system.

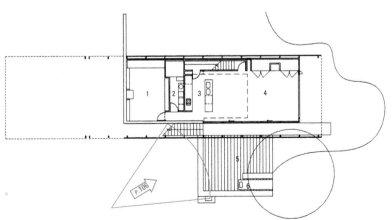

LOWER FLOOR

1 library
2 bathroom
3 kitchen
4 living/dining
5 deck
6 grill/fireplace

P.106

Architecture is a game of abstraction and proportion. Early architects considered mathematics a divine language: the palaces, public squares and temples of the Greeks and Romans are all based on sacred geometry of perfect squares and circles and their corresponding volumes of cubes and spheres. This is true for modern architecture, whose practitioners stripped away decorative motifs to reveal the essential geometric forms. Le Corbusier famously pronounced architecture to be the "magnificent play of volumes seen in light." But architecture is not constructed from volume and light alone; materials that constitute the lines, planes, and volumes of architectural forms add tangible depth and tactility that make celestial forms of geometry earthbound and rooted. At the Villa Eila, by Finnish architects Heikkinen-Komonen, the interplay of abstract volumes and tactile materials make for a serious and sensuous architecture.

Built on the outskirts of the town Mali for the founder of a Finnish not-for-profit organization, the Villa Eila employs local materials and building techniques of West Africa for this modest house. A series of free-standing volumes, circular or rectangular in plan, are set along a leveled foundation on the gently-sloped site. The geometric, independent rooms are constructed from stabilized earth, a local technique similar to rammed-earth in which cement and dry grass are mixed in with the moistened earth and molded into blocks. By utilizing this construction method, the architects avoided using costly transported materials or burnt brick, which has led to deforestation and contributed to the destabilizing of the region's delicate ecosystem. The blocks are natural thermodynamic containers, slowly retaining heat from the daytime to provide warmth at night, minimizing the fluctuation of the temperature inside the rooms and therefore eliminating the need for artificial heat. The discrete rooms are unified under a canopy, which is covered with thin roof tiles also made on-site.

Heikkinen-Komonen Architects
MALI, GUINEA **VILLA EILA** +

The western facade of the house is left open, facing a garden of fruit trees and blooming bushes, while the eastern facade is constructed of woven bamboo, creating a privacy wall but allowing light to filter in.

By employing local, "low-tech" building techniques and materials of the region, the architects designed an environmentally-sensitive house. At the same time, they reinvested the local architecture with the timeless spirit of architecture's essence.

LEFT + The African sunlight is dramatically filtered through the woven bamboo screen, animating the geometric forms of the Villa Eila.

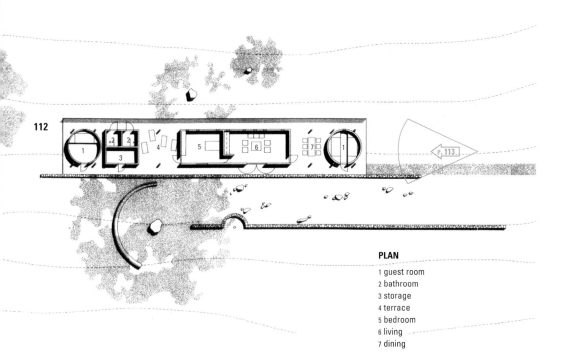

P. 113

PLAN

1 guest room
2 bathroom
3 storage
4 terrace
5 bedroom
6 living
7 dining

ABOVE + The discrete volumes of the Villa Eila are constructed from a local method similar to rammed-earth, utilizing indigenous construction materials. **OVERLEAF +** The separate rooms of the house are tied together by the overhanging roof.

Perhaps arising out of an instinct for survival, we often feel the urge to control our surroundings. Rivers are rerouted and mountains blasted to satisfy our need to master the forces of nature. But less violent engagements with nature can occur, and often on more satisfying terms. A more sympathetic and respectful dialog between nature and architecture takes an unexpected and delightful turn in the Dyngby House.

Designed by the young Danish architect Claus Hermansen, the Dyngby House functions mainly as a summer and weekend home. Taking advantage of the house's vacation usage, the architect plays with the iconography of house and our sense of scale. Two "house" volumes, complete with symmetrically pitched roofs, are placed at an angle to each other, one containing the living spaces, the other housing the bedrooms. A third space, with the entry hall and bathroom, bridges the two larger forms. Constructed from simple timber frames, the two "houses" are actually single-story spaces scaled down accordingly, lending the project a miniature, whimsical aspect that is found in vacation homes of the region. Inside, spaces are left open where possible and extraneous details are eliminated so that a sense of spaciousness prevails. In both volumes, large openings are cut into the walls, and glazed surfaces are inserted to allow light to enter.

Despite its relative proximity to the seafront, the Dyngby House's rectangular site is suburban in context, with neighboring houses within view. To deflect visual intrusion, the architect made an unexpected yet appropriate move by wrapping an oxidized steel mesh over the whole form of the house. Vines are then allowed to grown onto this screen, covering and hiding the house from nearby neighbors, with the camouflaging effects experienced both inside and outside. On the exterior, the neatly trimmed, leafy surfaces of the house are reminiscent of something out of Hans Christian Andersen, while on the interior, light filtered through the screen of leaves creates an otherworldly effect.

DYNGBY, DENMARK **DYNGBY HOUSE** +
Claus Hermansen Architects

Parts of the mesh enclosure surrounding the windows and sliding-glass doors are made into hinged openings, which can be unshuttered to allow direct light and air inside. When not in use, the house closes up, leaving only a verdant apparition that fades into the surrounding landscape.

RIGHT + The leafy vines growing on the Dyngby House allow it to blend into the verdant surroundings in the summer.

TOP + An oxidized steel mesh is hung off the conventional wood stud construction of the house. **RIGHT +** The mesh allows the passing seasons to determine the density and coloration of the leafy envelope.

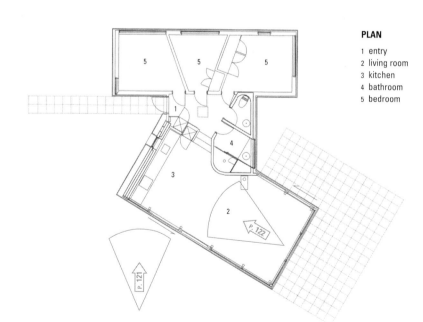

PLAN

1 entry
2 living room
3 kitchen
4 bathroom
5 bedroom

P. 122

P. 121

ABOVE ✚ At night the house glows through the mesh, revealing the structure underneath. **OVERLEAF ✚** The house's interiors are finished in warm materials and light colors traditional to the Scandinavian summer cottages.

The culture and population of Malaysia is a mélange of Malay, Chinese, and Indian, reflecting the country's historic role as a crossroads of trade and commerce. This history, and the influence of globalism, have produced a unique society, where the traditional and hyper-modern are sometimes incongruously juxtaposed, and sometimes seamlessly melded. Architecture here, likewise, can be seen as a combination of influences; layers of building cultures laminated together to produce new combinations. Concern for cultural conservation is leading to historical and stylistic pastiche. A few practitioners, however, have successfully and artfully wed local traditions and techniques to modern forms and construction. Their complex, thoughtful buildings embody the region's heritage without using stylistic gimmickry.

Kerry Hill Architects

Kerry Hill, a local architect based in Singapore, has a track record of producing modern buildings that reflect the cultural conditions and climate of tropical Asia. Drawing from vernacular architecture of the region, Hill also refers to structures built in Malaysia by European settlers over a century ago, which are now an integral part of the built landscape.

Using the breezeway as an organizing principle, the Mirzan House is a complex series of semi-detached buildings connected by a covered outdoor gallery. The spacious gallery connects the house from one end to the other in a direct linear path. The functions of the house are also divided by this same line, with the living quarters on one side, and the service spaces on the other. The material palette is equally clear. Masonry is employed at the ground level, while wood is used for the second floor exterior. Pitched roofs recall plantation homes of the region, but their form is also well-suited to withstand tropical storms. Water is also used judiciously, with rectangular ponds interspersed along the gallery. The reflective and flickering water surfaces provide visual interest, but their main function is to cool the exterior walkway.

In the Mirzan House, Kerry Hill expresses the regional character not through visual metaphors but through all the senses. Touch, sound, as well as sight, are required to experience this complex and unique architecture.

125

LEFT + A covered breezeway acts as the organizing spine and allows for exterior circulation between the different parts of the Mirzan House.

127

LEFT, ABOVE + Local materials of stone and wood and the use of pitched roofs reflect the traditional architecture of Malaysia.

TOP + A porte-cochere shades visitors from the intense sun. **RIGHT, OVERLEAF +** Shallow pools of water cool down the exterior breezeway.

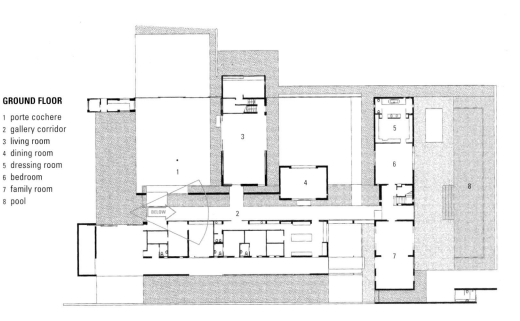

GROUND FLOOR

1 porte cochere
2 gallery corridor
3 living room
4 dining room
5 dressing room
6 bedroom
7 family room
8 pool

built up outside the living space to frame the view of the lake and block a public road that fronts the water. The ground floor, which is partially built into the slope of the site, contains the living spaces and kitchen. On the second floor, bedrooms, bathrooms, and private studies are simply arranged.

Vincent James Architect
✚ **DAYTON HOUSE** MINNEAPOLIS, UNITED STATES

At first glance, the Dayton House appears to be a classic modern house. Its crisp detailing and interplay of solid and void are further enhanced by the use of honed stone, large expanses of glass, and a cultivated landscape. Indeed, in form and in spirit, the house recalls the spatial serenity of Modernism's heyday. Examined in plan, though, the house tells a different story. House and landscape intermingle, overlap, and suffuse one another. Unlike its predecessors, whose glass walls are fixed, the Dayton House's flexible walls allow the structure to breath.

Architect Vincent James worked closely with the landscape architect George Hargreaves to finely calibrate the siting of the house on its suburban lot. Situated near a lake, the architect oriented the L-shaped house along the contour lines of the downward slope to capture the view of the natural landscape while blocking views of the neighboring houses. Designed for Minnesota's harsh winter months as well as its more temperate summer season, the main living spaces are sheathed in several layers: glass curtain walls, teak-slatted panels, and mosquito screens, all operable to modulate light, air, and views. Immediately beyond the house structure, terraces of grass and groves of trees are sited as outdoor rooms, deftly weaving the landscaping in with the interior spaces. A bermed terrace is

The flexible nature of the Dayton House serves its owners well, a retired couple who are very active in the local art and cultural community. The house is meant to host formal receptions as well as accommodate visits from the couple's grandchildren.

The owners are also collectors of modern art, especially sculpture, and artworks are carefully installed inside and outside the house. The result is a house that is woven into a cultivated site, blurring the line between architecture and landscape; a house that opens out to its surroundings, and breathes in the landscape.

133

LEFT ✚ The stately material palette of limestone, glass, and polished teak belies the Dayton House's flexible nature.
OVERLEAF ✚ The private spaces of the second floor are clad in stone, while the more public ground floor is sheathed in glass.

135

ABOVE + A paved courtyard at the front of the house acts as a motorcourt for visitors. **RIGHT** + Modern sculptures are carefully placed in the cultivated gardens, which are treated as outdoor rooms.

FIRST FLOOR

1 motor court
2 lawn
3 garage
4 sculpture grove
5 kitchen
6 dining
7 living
8 porch

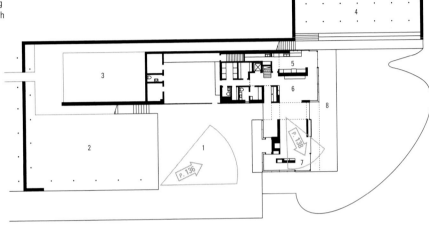

ABOVE ✛ The glass walls of the living room slide back to unite the house with the landscape. **RIGHT ✛** Teak shutters throughout the house subtly modulate sunlight and introduce the breezes from the nearby lake.

Chile is said to have more coastline per capita than any other country in the world. The country is composed of a thin strip of land stretching over 2,500 miles along the Pacific Ocean, and Chileans consider beach-front property almost a national right. This phenomenon, together with Chile's rich architectural heritage, has consequently produced beach houses on a scale and level of sophistication virtually unmatched.

Mathias Klotz Architect
+ **HOUSE 75** CANTAGUA, CHILE

At the forefront is the young architect Mathias Klotz, who has built an international reputation based on a series of waterfront houses. Starting with his own home–a severe, geometric volume that sits lightly on its site–Klotz has steadily evolved a language of wood, glass, crisp details, and clear structure that is deeply rooted in the visual and constructional tenets of Modernism yet is also unmistakably part of the local landscape.

In his latest project, House 75, Klotz has returned to his favorite plan type, the bar house. Located in a small town north of Chile's capital

Santiago, the site is a beautiful lot sloping gently towards the ocean. Following the client's request that every room have a view of the ocean, Klotz devised a series of rooms set parallel to the waterfront and interspersed with open spaces–in effect, creating a linear, subdivided terrace. This main living level is lifted off the ground on thin concrete piers, making the house appear to hover on its site while affording great views. To provide privacy as well as protection from the afternoon sun, a series of movable wood screens can be rolled out on tracks to shade the entire western facade.

Interior walls are eliminated wherever possible, or glazed with large panels of glass to maintain a sense of expansiveness. Appropriate for a dwelling near the ocean, both floors and ceilings are finished in a dark wood reminiscent of ship decking.

A shallow, ramplike set of stairs located along the back side of the house leads from the ground floor up to the living level, and then up again to a large open roof terrace. In effect, House 75, with its tri-partite zones, raised living level, circulation ramp, and rooftop terrace, can be interpreted as a loose homage to Le Corbusier's Villa Savoie. But unlike Le Corbusier's early masterpiece, which conspicuously occupies the crest of its site like the prow of a ship, House 75 is a more gentle vessel, attuned to the quiet, shifting currents of daily living.

RIGHT + House 75 is raised up on columns to provide the main living level an unobstructed view of the ocean. The structure is crisply detailed in steel, wood, and concrete.

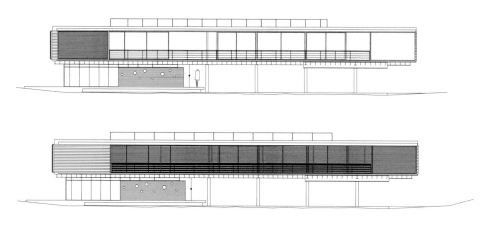

TOP, RIGHT + The western facade of the house can be closed off with a series of rolling wood shutters to block the afternoon sun and provide visual privacy.

ABOVE + A ramplike set of steps occupies the back of the house, provide exterior circulation between the three levels.
RIGHT + The floors and ceilings of the light-filled interiors are finished in a rich, dark wood reminiscent of ship decking.

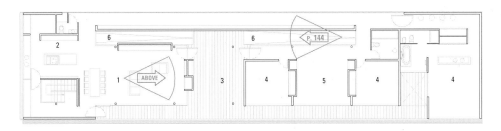

MAIN FLOOR

1 living/dining
2 kitchen
3 terrace
4 bedroom
5 family room
6 ramp

Glass, perhaps more than any other material, is intimately tied to modern architecture. Technological innovations in sheet-glass manufacturing at the turn of the 20th century, combined with the emerging new aesthetic for spatial and visual freedom, pushed glass to the forefront of the Modernist aesthetic. Almost 100 years later, the glass house continues to fascinate architects and their clients.

In the Laminata House, the role glass usually plays in building construction has been turned, literally. The result of a competition held by a glass manufacturer in the Netherlands, the Laminata House is a bold experiment that employ glass as a structural material, but it also addresses issues that have plagued glass construction from its earliest days–privacy and security. The winning team of Paul van der Erve and Gerald Kruunenberg worked closely with the glass manufacturer and outside consultants to realize their design.

Conceptually, the house is composed of a solid block of glass that has been laminated from individual layers, out of which the rooms and spaces are then carved. In reality, over 10,000 separate sheets of glass are cut precisely to individual unique sizes then cleaned on site and glued together to form massive walls. Many technical considerations are taken into account in the delicate construction. "The whole process was like working in a laboratory," Paul van der Erve commented. Electrical and heating systems, which usually employ walls as conduits, are imbedded into the concrete foundation floor. Other challenges, such as the expansion rate of the naturally brittle glass, required more hi-tech solutions in the form of a silicon-based glue that is permanently flexible.

LEERDAM, THE NETHERLANDS **LAMINATA HOUSE +**
Kruuneberg van der Erve Architects

The result is an astonishing visual feat, unlike any other glass house ever built. The thinness of glass panes gives way to substantial, ice-like volumetric masses, which the architects accentuate by giving the interior walls an undulating footprint. Laminated together, the fragile sheet glass takes on incredible strength, and can withstand direct force at the same level as concrete. Its thickness also absorbs all heat gain, eliminating the need for a cooling system.

After a period when it was opened to public viewing, the house was purchased by an artist couple for their own residence and studio. Fortuitously, the architects provided for a ceiling-mounted system for hanging the owners' art. Even without it, the Laminata House stands as an artwork itself.

147

LEFT + The main hallway of the Laminata House showcases the innovative use of glass as a structural material: individual glass panes are laminated together to form the thick walls.

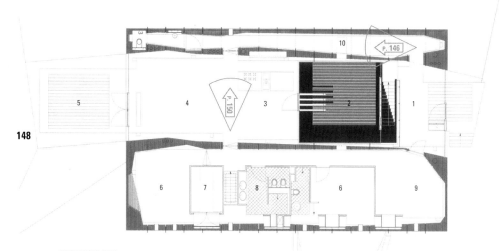

P. 146

P. 150

GROUND FLOOR

1 entry	6 bedroom
2 open to below	7 closet
3 kitchen	8 bathroom
4 living/dining	9 study
5 terrace	10 corridor

TOP, RIGHT + Although the main facade of the house is composed purely of glass, the material takes on unusual characteristics of opacity and strength not normally associated with glass walls.

LEFT + Due to the impermeable glass walls of the Laminata House , electrical conduits are imbedded into the concrete floor.
ABOVE + A clerestory around an interior courtyard bring direct light into the house.

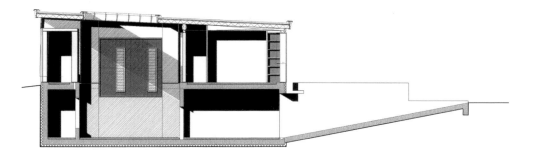

LEFT + The central courtyard extends downward to the garage and studio spaces at the basement level. **ABOVE +** The thick, translucent glass walls have the same insulation properties as more conventional building construction.

Anupama Kundoo, in designing a house for herself, has eschewed state-of-the-art technologies that often preoccupy younger architects. Rather, she has chosen to investigate local building traditions in India with the explicit aim of building an eco-friendly dwelling.

Located near the eastern coast of India, Kundoo's Wall House is located in the town of Auroville, an utopian experiment in living. Established in 1968 with the authorization of the government, Auroville operates as an independent entity—with its own charter and jurisdiction—and has drawn participants from over thirty countries to form an international community dedicated to creating alternative methods of working and living. These activities range from organic agriculture to new forms of information technology; a sustainable architecture is an integral part of this experiment.

154 AUROVILLE, INDIA **WALL HOUSE** +
Anupama Kundoo

As its name implies, the Wall House is a series of spaces arranged along a spine. This central structure, constructed from locally produced brick, is oriented to the southeast for optimal air circulation, while the double-height volume enhances vertical ventilation. Material efficiency is achieved through the use of hollow clay tubes to construct the vault roof, and use of cement is minimized by inserting terra-cotta pots into the concrete floorings. While solid on one side, the structure opens out on the other side, clad only in wooden grilles that block the afternoon sun while allowing air and views to freely penetrate. Discrete spaces can be closed with shutters, although no part of the house is noise- or air-tight. By using both traditional and contemporary construction techniques and building strategies, the Wall House eliminate the need for outside power, and relies solely on electricity generated by photovoltaic cells for water heating and water pumping.

The Wall House is a seamless blend of ancient and modern. It successfully employs the language of Modernism and revives ancient construction methods to present a fresh alternative for the house of tomorrow.

RIGHT + The Wall House incorporates local building traditions and materials to produce an ecologically-friendly dwelling.

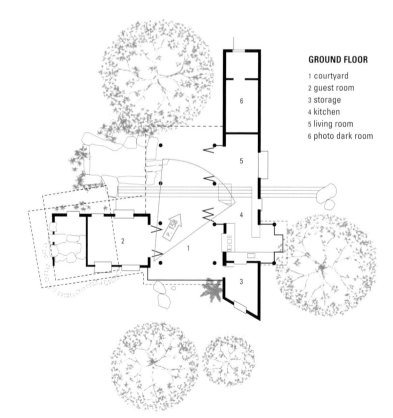

GROUND FLOOR

1 courtyard
2 guest room
3 storage
4 kitchen
5 living room
6 photo dark room

LEFT ✛ The house faces southeast to take advantage of the natural airflow. **ABOVE ✛** All rooms open directly to the natural surroundings. **OVERLEAF ✛** The modern, exposed concrete structure is combined with more traditional brick walls to create a visual complex space.

The intergenerational family house is common everywhere in the world except the United States and Europe. Taking many forms in different cultures, the cohabitation of grandparents, parents, and children is an ancient tradition. The shared communal spaces of the intergenerational house—with separate private spaces for couples or individuals—allow more opportunities for family members from different generations to interact with one another. The rich and layered relationships that results are more typical of what one finds in a small village, and not what one encounters in the single generation, nuclear family homes of your average suburban development. Raveevarn Choksombatchai and Ralph Nelson of LOOM Studio have seized on this phenomenon in their design of the Unfolding House.

Built in a busy residential neighborhood of Bangkok, the Unfolding House turns inward, taking its cues from the traditional courtyard house. From the interior, a series of rooms open up sequentially. The architects cite the Asian folding screen painting as a spatial paradigm for the house, noting that we "rarely experience architecture as a clear and distinct whole, but rather as a series of continually unfolding events." LOOM Studio configured the house so that spaces are experienced according to time and movement.

To combat the tropical sun, walls opening into the courtyard are clad in brises-soleil—concrete screens that block the direct sun but allow for an even, reflected light to enter. Major openings are strategically placed to take advantage of the prevailing breezes, and windows can be opened and adjusted to modulate air flow. The inverted, butterfly roofs allow for natural air circulation, and capture rainwater that is used to cool the house and is then drained into holding cisterns for household uses.

BANGKOK, THAILAND **UNFOLDING HOUSE** +
LOOM Studio

Construction is cast-in-place concrete, currently the most common building material in the region, with wood used as partition walls, flooring, and finishes. While concrete is a relatively new material in the context of Thailand's deep-rooted architectural heritage, by using it simply and directly, the architects embrace the spirit of traditional construction which always reveals the true building method and materials. In many ways, though, the most important material in the Unfolding House is light itself: modulated, screened, and otherwise transformed. The day's light, as it ebbs and flows, tracks time and movement along the house's unfolding spaces, illuminating the memories and history of family members residing within.

LEFT + The Unfolding House is sheathed in concrete screens to shade the cool interiors from the strong tropical sunlight.

162

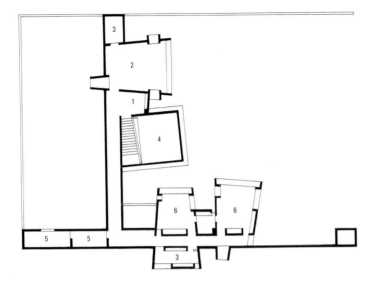

SECOND FLOOR

1 pray room
2 master bedroom
3 bathroom
4 open to below
5 laundry
6 bedroom
7 study

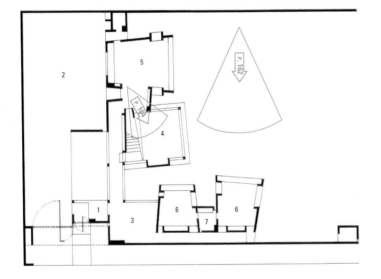

FIRST FLOOR

1 entry
2 car port
3 entrance hall
4 living room
5 kitchen/dining
6 bedroom
7 bathroom

LEFT + All living spaces, including the double-height living room, contain operable windows to take advantage of the natural air circulation.

TOP + The intimate dining room constrasts with the grand living space beyond. **RIGHT +** The tranquil outdoor room is actually the laundry washing area on the second floor.

The Australian architect Glenn Murcutt is known for his precise, sparse (though never severe), and often unassuming houses that utilize materials found in local vernacular buildings—such as corrugated tin and thin wood members—to produce an architecture rooted to the region and at the same time to advance the language of Modernism.

Located in a rural site outside of Sydney, the Kangaroo Valley House sits on a leveled area in a gently sloping landscape. Like many of Murcutt's houses, the Kangaroo Valley House is a slender, single story with a pitched roof. Although a self-proclaimed Modernist, Murcutt often employs the pitched roof in his buildings, a necessity in the rainy region and therefore the simplest solution. At the Kangaroo Valley House, the angle of the roof mimics the slope of the ground, and water collected from the roof on rainy days drains into holding reservoirs beside the house for later use. The length of the structure is oriented east/west; the entry is on the taller side of the pitched roof, while the opposite side faces a national park. Rooms are laid out linearly according to use, with the master bedroom, bathroom and a combined living/dining/kitchen space located in one half of the house. The other half houses a guest room with bathroom, a studio, and garage. The combined living/dining/kitchen is the largest room in the house, although it is the same single-room width as the rest of the

structure. Instead of making this space wider, Murcutt instead takes advantage of the temperate climate of the region by installing a series of large rolling window walls of mosquito netting, wooden shutters, and corrugated metal. Each set can be opened or closed depending on the user's needs. With the walls completely open, the living space extends out to the landscape in an unbroken sequence.

Glenn Murcutt Architect
NEW SOUTH WALES, AUSTRALIA **KANGAROO VALLEY HOUSE** ✚

The single-room depth and the single story height of the house also encourage the use of exterior spaces as circulation. In addition to the main entrance, two doors at either ends are also used as access points. The exterior construction is brick, with partial wood cladding, sitting on top of a thin concrete foundation. A clerestory is installed at the high side of the pitched roof to allow northern sunlight to enter during the winter months, a motif that is brought into the interior partition walls as well. The house is finished and furnished simply, in keeping with the overall intention of the architecture.

LEFT ✚ The unassuming Kangaroo Valley House nestles gently into its rural site near Sydney. The linear plan allows for views in all directions from each room of the house.

LEFT, ABOVE + The single-room width of the house encourages the use of exterior spaces; the pitched roof collects water for household use.

173

ABOVE ✦ The southern facade is a series of rolling doors that open the house to its natural surroundings.

PLAN

1 porch
2 master bedroom
3 kitchen/dining/living
4 entry
5 guest room
6 studio
7 garage
8 cisterns

ABOVE + The combined living/dining/kitchen space of the Kangaroo Valley house is at once utilitarian and inviting.
RIGHT + Clerestory windows on the north facade allow sunlight to warm the house during the winter.

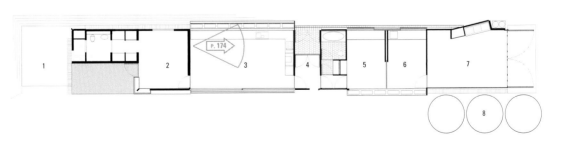

P. 174

The prototype house has a long and illustrious history in modern architecture. Throughout its history, the prototype house's agenda has fluctuated with the social concerns of the day. At the Weissenhof Exhibition of 1927 at Stuttgart, Germany, the overriding goal was to provide housing for the working class. The Case Study Houses in California promoted open-plan living and the use of industrial materials—especially off-the-shelf steel—in residential construction. Many housing prototypes seem hopelessly naive (almost all "houses of the future" at World Fairs), while others, such as Buckminster Fuller's Dymaxion House, remain visionary propositions. Kazuhiko Namba's Eco-Aluminum House is one of the latest to join the architectural prototype lineage.

Kazuhiko Namba + KAI Workshop

TSUKUBA, JAPAN **ECO-ALUMINUM HOUSE** ✛

In this project Namba focused on the use of aluminum as a viable building material. Aluminum is a relatively "modern" material, although its raw form, aluminum oxide, is the most abundant element in the earth's upper crust. For a long time the extraction of pure aluminum out of its raw state was a laborious and costly endeavor, yielding very little final product. A technological breakthrough at the end of the 19th century opened the floodgates for aluminum's ubiquity in modern life, and although it is the leading non-corrosive metal in use, very little aluminum is found in building construction. The Eco-Aluminum House tests aluminum's unique properties: it is lightweight, rustproof, easy to manufacture, and recyclable.

Using the traditional Japanese house idea of the module as a starting point, Namba calculated the new module by determining the maximum span of aluminum. Various configurations of the module were then designed, with the final house taking the form of the nine-square grid: living spaces centered around an open courtyard.

Except for certain finishes, all parts of the house, including the structure, exterior cladding, and roof, are made from aluminum parts, all fabricated offsite and assembled at the building site with mechanical fasteners; no welding is needed, eliminating an expensive necessity on most steel jobs. The result is a lightweight structure that is easily manufactured and transported, employing a strong but affordable, recyclable material. By using the traditional courtyard house type, Namba was able to dispel notions that modular, pre-fabricated houses are not livable. In fact, the Eco-Aluminum House is a light, airy structure of well-proportioned spaces and precise detailing. It's well-thought out layout distinguishes it from past prototypes, where new—and often ill-conceived—notions of space were implemented. This is one idea that doesn't need to be recycled.

RIGHT ✛ A mature tree anchors the open courtyard of the Eco-Aluminum House, a new housing prototype that explores alumnum as an alternative construction material.

GROUND FLOOR

1 courtyard
2 dining/kitchen
3 living room
4 bathroom
5 guest room

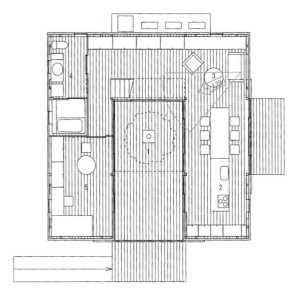

TOP + The nine-square grid plan of the house is based on the traditional Japanese concept of the housing module.
RIGHT+ The living spaces face inward to the open interior couryard.

SECOND FLOOR

1 family room
2 bedroom
3 study
4 bathroom

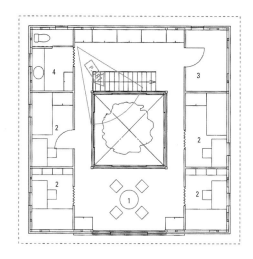

LEFT + The living room, dining room, and kitchen are housed on the ground floor, with the bedrooms located on the second level.
TOP + Except for certain finishes, all parts of the house are constructed from aluminum.

the living area as well as a photography studio. The roof gently bows, diffusing both natural and artificial light, while the all-glass western wall can be shuttered to provide absolute darkness. When not in use as a photo studio, the space is a dramatic living room that extends to the garden outside and the spectacular view beyond.

Before the existence of written language and the printed book, buildings were the primary means to preserve knowledge and memory. The repositories were tombs, memorials to heroes and rulers, but also temples, churches, civic buildings, and even private houses. The cathedral at Chartres is more than a place of worship for its builders. For the mostly illiterate population, the stained-glass windows were parables of good and evil, of pain and joy. Even after a building is gone, some remnants can still remain, a column or a painted sign, which can trigger memories not only of the lost building, but also of its inhabitants. Aware of the power of architecture to evoke memory, the owner of the Light House requested that a remnant wall from the previous house be kept and incorporated into the new design, as a reminder and touchstone of the house's previous inhabitant, a good friend of the client.

The architectural firm of Olson Sundberg Kundig Allen used the foundation of the previous house as a starting basis, but rotated the new plan at a slight angle to take full advantage of the Puget Sound views. The entry is where old and new meet, with the remnant wall and the new front wall creating an open slot where the house is entered. The main space of the house is a sweeping double-height structure that is used as

+ LIGHT HOUSE SEATTLE, WASHINGTON
Olson Sundberg Kundig Allen Architects

While the front and side walls are solid concrete construction, the back wall employs both beefy steel members and smaller, more delicate mullions and stanchions to create a composed, impressive wall of steel and glass. To further enhance the industrial nature of the space, the large I-beams are left unfinished, to age naturally with the house. In contrast, finely honed and precisely finished furnishings in steel and wood were created by local craftsmen especially for the space. Behind the open kitchen is the master bedroom suite, where the same exact and loving details are employed in the custom fixtures and vanity.

By superimposing the new house on the old without eradicating it, the Light House becomes the new repository of the collective history of the site, which will continues to accumulate as the house ages.

185

LEFT + The Light House is located on a strip of land on the Puget Sound, one of the Pacific Northwest's most spectacular settings.

186

TOP ✚ Composed of large, exposed steel beams, the main facade is infilled with mostly glass to take in the panoramic views.
RIGHT ✚ The new, cast-in-place structure contrasts nicely with the old rubble, remnant wall from the old house on the site.
OVERLEAF ✚ The main living space is an airy, double-height space that doubles as a photography studio for the owner.

GROUND FLOOR

1 entry
2 living/dining
3 terrace
4 kitchen
5 study
6 bedroom
7 dressing room
8 bathroom
9 garage

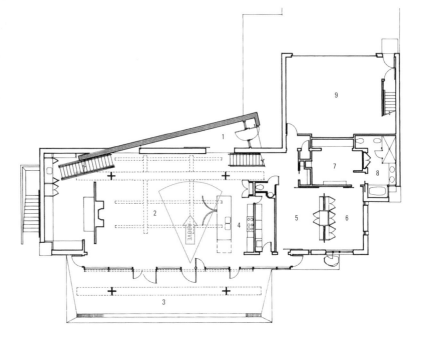

TOP + All the furniture and furnishings, such as the steel candelabra, were designed and fabricated by local craftsmen to complement the unique architecture. **RIGHT +** The industrial feel of the house continues in the master bathroom, with the use of cast-in-place concrete for the tub and stainless steel for the sink vanity.

The play of transparency and opacity is a visual and structural game of continual interest. Contemporary architects often use screening devices of wood, metal, and fabric to filter light and alter visibility. Only rarely, though, is water used as the filtering agent. The Vancouver House, located on a narrow site in a dense suburban context, achieves opacity outwardly and horizontally, but maintains transparency inwardly and vertically, partly through a floating body of water.

✚ VANCOUVER HOUSE VANCOUVER, CANADA
Patkau Architects

Following the client's request, Patkau Architects resolved the difficult feat of fitting a lap pool in the 33-foot wide site by hoisting it into the air. In plan the elongated pool on the second floor hovers over the entry walkway of the first floor plan, leaving as much room as possible for the living spaces at ground level. On the tight site, which presents spectacular views of the Vancouver skyline, the architects had nowhere to build but vertically, which they did

by excavating a partial basement for a music room and creating double-height volumes in the living spaces. Light reflecting off the lap pool is captured and reflected through the clerestory window to a light scoop and brought down to the dining room below, granting the space daylight even in the darkest winter days. The most dramatic effect produced by the pool, however, is at the entry of the house, where the sunlight piercing through the pool's glass bottom animates and lightens every surface. A swimmer in the pool can clearly see any visitors, and vice-versa. To make the floating pool possible structurally and to meet earthquake building codes, the architects employed a heavily reinforced concrete structure. Some of the concrete piers are left exposed inside, constantly reminding the inhabitants of the forces holding up the fifty-ton pool above.

The complex and robust structure, combined with the architects' complex configuration of the living spaces—all designed to bring in the maximum amount of light into every part of the house—resulted in an interior that John Patkau describes as "both minimal and baroque." For all of its visual and constructional complexity, the house exudes serenity, utilizing the reflective light as visual white noise, and contrasting its own verticality with expansive horizontal views.

RIGHT ✚ At the Vancouver House, sunlight is transformed into flickering patterns as it penetrates through the floating pool's glass bottom.

LEFT + Squeezed into a narrow lot, the house expands linearly and vertically. **ABOVE** + The different levels of the complex interior are connected with a series of steps. **OVERLEAF** + The living room's glass walls are angled to capture the panoramic view of the city beyond.

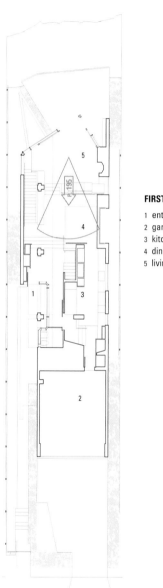

FIRST FLOOR

1 entry
2 garage
3 kitchen
4 dining room
5 living room

SECOND FLOOR

1 deck
2 bedroom
3 bathroom
4 open to below
5 study
6 terrace
7 pool

RIGHT + At night the lap pool's crystal clear surface acts as a lens to the house entry immediately below it; the pool visually connect to the bay beyond.

The basic relationship between architecture and landscape represents our evolving attitude toward nature. It is now untenable to privilege the building over its site. Architecture and landscape, as equal partners, can produce a deeper and more meaningful environment. The Karjat Farmhouse, by Samira Rathod, is an example of building and site working together to produce a richer experience.

The house's site is located approximately sixty miles outside of Bombay, on a lush plateau overlooking a lake. Respecting the mature trees already on the land, Rathod devised a plan composed of a series of walls that weave in between and around the trees. Consequently, it is hard to visualize the house as a discrete whole. Rather, the house, the trees, and the surrounding landscape are meant to be understood as a single entity. "At the end, what was important to me was to camouflage the house into the surroundings to allow the birds that flock there before construction began to continue doing so," Rathod says.

As one approaches the house, which is partly hidden by the trees, the ground begins to change from dirt and gravel to smooth stone paving, with trees located where they were before construction. Entering the house through the entry court, the visitor encounters a series of semi-enclosed spaces—more open than a room but more contained than a courtyard. These spaces are built around two existing trees, which interrupt the house's structure and break free above, giving the impression that the house has been there for a long time. Defined on two sides by stuccoed brick walls, the house is fenestrated with large openings which provide framed views of the landscape beyond. The third wall is mostly glass, while the fourth is an interior wall that delimits the large living room from a bedroom located behind it. The bedroom suite is raised slightly above the living level, although there is no sound barrier between the spaces. Beyond the living room is a terrace, which becomes part of the living space as soon as the large glass partitions are pulled back.

A color palette of muted browns and blues soften the house, blending with the colors of the landscape, while the stuccoed brick walls support a series of metal trusses that give the main living space a sense of structural lightness.

The Karjat Farmhouse is small, but by engaging the surrounding landscape around it both physically and visually, it becomes much larger than its footprint.

201

LEFT + By weaving the new house around the existing mature trees on the site, The Karjat Farmhouse gives the impression of being a much older structure.

GROUND FLOOR

1 entry
2 kitchen
3 dining
4 living
5 bedroom
6 bathroom

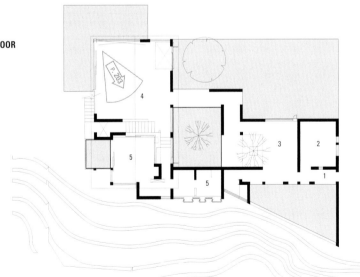

LEFT + The house weaves dicreetly between the mature trees on the site. **ABOVE +** The thin metal trusses, corrugated tin roof, and stone floor are typical of the area's farm structure.

ABOVE + The bedroom area, raised on a mezzanine, is immediately behind the main living room. **RIGHT +** The glass walls of the house roll back to unite the living room with the terrace and views of the majestic mountain range beyond.

The automobile is an integral part of modern life, yet its relationship to buildings, especially residential architecture, has never been fully resolved. At best, garages are placed on the side or back of the house, hidden from view so as not to sully the architecture; or at worst—as in the case of suburban tract homes—positioned front and center yet devoid of character or formal qualities. When the automobile and architecture meet fortuitously, the results can be striking. In a visionary project by Michael Webb of the English architectural group Archigram, cars move along tracks then climb buildings and become integrated into the architecture itself. At the Cheval Place, this spirit of harmonious coexistence of car and architecture lives on.

The Cheval Place is a small pied-a-terre for a car collector. As the house is located on a small alleyway in London, street parking is an impossibility. Unwilling to part with any of his prized autos, the client requested a two-car garage on the tiny lot. To manage this feat, and leave room for the living spaces, the architect Seth Stein responded to the unusual request by ingeniously employing technology used for parking cars in city garages—the car lift—to turn parking space into living space, and vice-versa. The basement level is excavated to house the living areas, which are arranged on two levels, one housing the kitchen and dining space, the other the living

LONDON, ENGLAND **CHEVAL PLACE** +
Seth Stein Architect

room. Directly above the living room is the lower deck of the car lift, with its double decks. In this upper position, the lower deck is at street level and is able to receive a car, while the space directly below is usable as the living room. When the occasion demands it, the lift is lowered, with the lower deck occupying the space of the living room and the upper deck ready to receive the second car.

With the car lift in the lowered position, the owner loses the living space, but gains a full view of a part of his collection. In keeping with the sleek lines of the cars, the interior is finished simply and efficiently, with a small bed and bath on the second floor. Frosted and clear glass are used judiciously, emphasizing the hide-and-seek nature of the lift. Although the Cheval Place makes witty and knowing allusions to London's recent architectural past, its intention and execution produce a winning example for the future relationship of the automobile and architecture.

207

LEFT + A pied-a-terre for a car collector, the Cheval Place is designed to showcase the owner's vintage automobiles. Skylights on the ground floor introduce light to the basement living level.

208

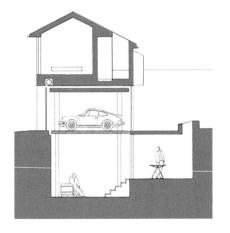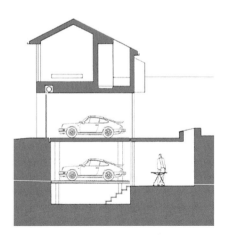

LEFT, ABOVE ✛ The ground floor garage is actually a carlift that can be lowered to accomodate a second vehicle above. Living spaces are housed at this basement level, while the bedroom and bathroom are located on the floor above the garage.

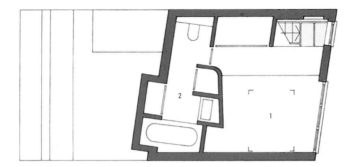

SECOND FLOOR

1 bedroom
2 bathroom

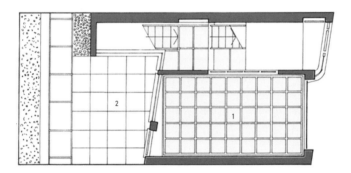

FIRST FLOOR

1 garage / carlift
2 terrace

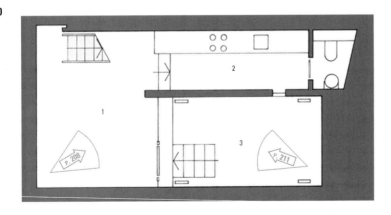

BASEMENT LEVEL

1 dining
2 kitchen
3 living / carlift above

RIGHT ✛ When not in use as a display/garage space, the room beneath the car lift doubles as additional living space.

The tree is a powerful symbol in many societies, but especially to indigenous African cultures. Representing life itself, trees provide sustenance, shade, and security. As the South African architects van der Merwe Miszewski have stated: "Trees are precious in Africa. In many ways the tree has become iconic, almost mythical." In designing the Tree House, the architects cited the majestic umbrella pines as their inspiration.

The site, a sloping site on the outskirts of Cape Town, is covered with the beautiful umbrella pines, a species rarely found outside of this region of the world. Tall and sculptural, the umbrella pine's canopy provides cool shade against the hot African sun. The Tree House' structure is composed of five tree-like columns extending from the ground upwards to anchor the roof. Steel columns support the lower floors like a tree trunk, and timber "branches" at their tops spread out to support the roof canopy.

The three levels of the Tree House form a tri-partite composition, with a base, middle, and top–each defined by different materials. The ground floor, which contains the garage, study, and guest room, is a brick structure clad with rusticated black slate. The second and third floor, housing the bedrooms, bathrooms, and a living/dining space, are sheathed in a steel and glass. The third compositional element, a floating roof, is a light timber frame.

The house can be entered on two levels. One entry is on the ground floor, on the lower side of the slope, while the other entry is on the third floor, accessed by a bridge that connects the higher side of the slope to the house. A circular stair clad in stainless steel is the vertical circulation connecting each level. Each floor of the rectangular plan is bisected by an undulating wall that mimics a stream running through the site. The wall weaves between the structural columns, adding another nature-inspired element.

By mimicking the form and function of the surrounding umbrella pines, the Tree House provides protection from the African sun while allowing the spectacular Table Mountain peaks to be viewed uninterrupted through the glass curtain walls of the house.

van der Merwe Miszewski Architects
+ **TREE HOUSE** CAPE TOWN, SOUTH AFRICA

RIGHT + Set against the spectacular Table Mountain in Cape Town, the Tree House's structure is inpired by the surrounding umbrella pines.

ABOVE ✛ The top floor is accessed by a bridge connecting the top of the sloped site to the house. RIGHT ✛ Access to all three floors is through a circular stair, emphasizing the verticality of the house. OVERLEAF ✛ The "branches" of the structural columns support the canopy roof of the open living space.

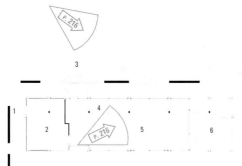

THIRD FLOOR

1 service stairs
2 kitchen
3 entrance bridge
4 open to below
5 living/dining area
6 terrace

FIRST FLOOR

1 driveway
2 garage
3 apartment
4 study
5 bedroom
6 pool

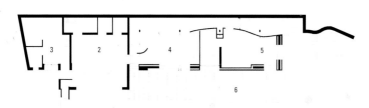

ABOVE + Private spaces such as the bedrooms are appropriately scaled down while retaining the same material palette of steel, glass, and wood.

Throughout history, artists have designed buildings, and designers have produced art. The Campidoglio, one of Rome's most breath-taking plazas, is the work of the artist Michelangelo. Today, Frank Gehry proudly proclaims his buildings as living sculptures. Ai Wei Wei, a Chinese artist best known for his constructed assembages, is squarely within this tradition. He designs spaces that are spare, minimal settings rich with subtle textures and the play of light.

Located outside of Beijing, the Studio House is set behind the wall of an open courtyard, following the local traditional architecture. The building, as viewed from the courtyard, though, is a severe composition of mostly blind facades, further enhancing the introspective nature of the house and its contents. Ai Wei Wei's sculptures, which slice apart antique Chinese furniture and reassemble them, reinterpret notions of tradition and modernity. In much the same way, the Studio House reassembles local material and construction within the crisp volumes of modern architecture. Although the building is a concrete structure, the exterior is clad with small, gray bricks, made locally and often used in the vernacular buildings of the region. Inside the tall envelope, the house is organized as a series of expansive double-height spaces, with the small second floor acting as a mezzanine level. The first large space is used as a living and dining room, with a set of concrete stairs wrapping along the back walls leading to the upper level. The artist's just-completed sculptures and works-in-progress are displayed within this space, but the bulk of the artworks is produced and displayed in the second large volume, accessed through a set of double-height doors. The studio is a large, rectangular room, and with the exception of the doors, the walls are completely blank. The severity of the space, however, is softened by the natural light coming from a large skylight in the ceiling. Here, in a space larger than most galleries, Wei Wei creates and displays his large installation pieces.

BEIJING, CHINA **STUDIO HOUSE** ✛

Ai Wei Wei

The process of making is considered by Wei Wei to be a part of his artistic output. The construction of the house itself was conducted as a performance/installation; local workers under the supervision of the artist built the house and studio in exactly one hundred days. Wei Wei explains his art and architecture as a process of stripping away the superflous–"To withdraw unnecessary temptations," in his words–to reveal the essence. Whether it results in a sculpture or a building is immaterial.

LEFT ✛ The stripped-down volumes of the Studio House are clad in gray brick, made locally and found throughout the region's vernacular architecture.

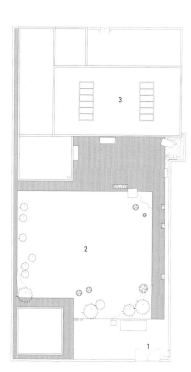

SITE PLAN

1 entry
2 courtyard garden
3 studio/house

ABOVE + The severe form of the Studio House belies the light, spacious interiors. **RIGHT** + The house entry also doubles as an exhibition space for the artist-owner's work-in-progress.

LEFT + Like an artist's urban loft, the interior's concrete structure and the red brick infill is left exposed.
ABOVE + Chinese antiques, an important source of inspiration for the artist, can be found throughout the house.

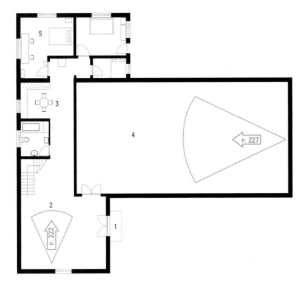

SECOND FLOOR

1 master bedroom
2 terrace
3 study
4 bathroom
5 open to below

FIRST FLOOR

1 entry
2 living room
3 dining room
4 studio
5 guest room

RIGHT + The large, serene studio provides ample space for the artist's art installations; the single skylight is the only source of illumination for the interior.

Good architecture is often rooted to a particular place; influenced by the physical site, the climate, the culture, and—most importantly—its people. A people's behavior, demeanor, and habits are translated into their buildings. Front porches in the American south are places to catch the evening breeze; but they also promote, and reinforce informal social interaction. Traditional Japanese houses often don't have bedrooms for individuals; the Japanese reticence does not extend to family members. It is clear that people and their behavior can affect their architecture, and arguably the reverse is equally true. The Stone Cloud House, by Kyo Sung Woo, investigates how architecture and human behavior influence each other.

Kyo Sung Woo Architect

The multi-generational family house is quite common in Seoul. The traditional Korean dwelling follows the inwardly-focused courtyard house typology, where living spaces on all four sides can be opened up to the communal activities within the private courtyard. In older cities this type works quite well, providing an open-air space in the tight maze of narrow streets and alleys. Currently, fewer of these courtyard houses are built in urban areas, where land is scarce. This is true of the Stone Cloud House, where the steep site precipitates a vertical as well as a horizontal building strategy. Anchored into the hillside, the Stone Cloud House rises up to five levels. Parking is on the ground floor, while the second floor contains a private apartment. The third floor is devoted to living spaces: kitchen, dining room, living room, a study, and the prerequisite outdoor courtyard, now lifted two stories above ground and overlooking the city. The fourth floor houses bedrooms, while the fifth floor is a terrace with panoramic views. The house is clad in honed stone, and the interiors are finished in a palette of warm woods, steel and glass.

The architect's open plan for the living level is not unusual; open, shared rooms wrapped around a courtyard is a common house type. But what is unique to this particular house is that Woo leaves the fourth side of the courtyard open, unoccupied by the house. To a Western visitor this seems logical, especially given the beautiful view afforded. Woo's reason for this move, however, is more sociological than scenographic. Korea's culture is characterized by introversion, as represented by the courtyard house, yet the rapid transformation of Korea's economic and social structures has coaxed people to be more "outwardly focused." By leaving the fourth wall out of the Stone Cloud House, Woo is literally leaving the house and its occupants open to outside influences.

LEFT + The Stone Cloud House is a modern interpretation of the traditional Korean house, where all living spaces are centered around an interior coutyard.

TOP ✛ The traditional coutyard of the vernacular Korean house is updated and now located on the third level of this five-story house. **RIGHT, OVERLEAF** ✛ Wood and glass stairs lead from the lower levels to the living room and up to the bedrooms.

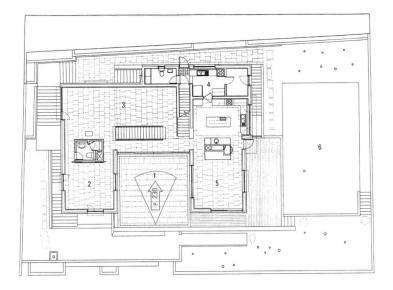

THIRD FLOOR

1 courtyard
2 study
3 living / dining
4 kitchen
5 family room
6 grass terrace

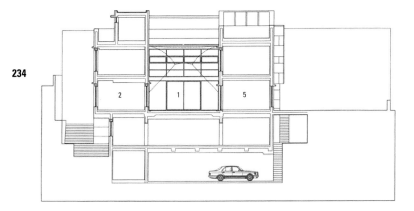

RIGHT + The rooftop level is a large terrace overlooking the city. The Stone Cloud House transforms the inwardly focused courtyard house model to an outwardly focused prototype by leaving one side open.

+ PROJECT AND
PHOTOGRAPHY CREDITS

Olga House, São Paulo, Brazil
Architect: Marcos Acayaba Arquitetos: Marcos Acayaba, Mauro Halluli, Edson Hiroyama, Tania Shirakawa, project team
Consultants: Helio Olga de Souza Jr., structural, electrical, and plumbing; Ita Constructora Ltda., wood structure fabrication and assembly
Contractor: Ita Constructora Ltda.
Photography: Nelson Kon

F-2 House, Mexico City, Mexico
Architect: Adria Broid Rojkind Arquitectos: Miquel Adria, Isaac Broid, Michel Rojkind, principals; Benjamin Campos, Andres Altesor, Agustin Pereyra, Miguel de Rio, Hernan Cuadra, Paulina Goycoolea, project team
Consultants: Salvador Mandujano, structural engineer; Antonio Valeriano, mechanical, electrical & plumbing
Contractors: Proyectos Alpha S.A. de C.V.; Jorge Abdel y Mauricio Abdel; Margaro Mendoza
Photography: Undine Prohl

Chicago House, Chicago, Illinois
Architect: Tadao Ando Architect & Associates: Tadao Ando, principal; Masataka Yano, project architect
Consultants: Booth/Hansen & Associates, architect of record; Clarkson Consulting, project management; Cohen Barreto Marchertas, Inc., structural engineer; Dickerson Engineering, electrical engineer; Brian Berg & Associates, mechanical engineer
Contractor: Zera Construction
Photography: Shigeo Ogawa

D'Allesandro House, São Paulo, Brazil
Architect: Andrade Morettin Arquitetos Associados: Vinicius Andrade & Marcelo Morettin, principals; J.G. da Silveira, J.E. Alves, project team
Consultants: ITA/Helio Olga, wood structure
Contractor: J. Francisco Chaves
Photography: Nelson Kon

Clifford House, Auckland, New Zealand
Architect: Architectus: Patrick Clifford, principal in charge; Malcolm Bowes, Michael Thomson, Mahendra Daji, James Fenton, Tim Mein, Rod Stellas, project team
Consultants: Brown & Thomson, structural engineers
Contractor: Trendsetter Builders
Photography: Patrick Reynolds, Paul McCreadie

Colorado House, Telluride, Colorado

Architect: Architecture Research Office: Stephen Cassell and Adam Yarinsky, partners in charge; John Quale, Scott Abrahams, Matt Azen, Tom Jenkinson, Monica Rivera, Martha Skinner, Kim Yao, Innes Yates, project team
Consultants: Mathews Nielsen Landscape Architecture; Burggraaf Associates (MEP); Buckhorn Geotech Engineers (structural consultant and septic engineer); Edison Price Architectural Lighting (lighting consultant); Reginald Hough (concrete consultant)
Contractor: Fortenberry Construction, Paul Ricks (project manager)

Split House, Yanquing, Beijing, China

Architect: Atelier Feichang Jianzhu: Yung Ho Chang, principal in charge; Liu Xianghui, Lu Xiang, Lucas Gallardo, Wang Hui, Xu Yixing, project team
Consultants: Xu Minsheng, structural engineers
Contractor: China Construction First Division [Group] The Fouth Construction Co.
Photography: Fu Xing

Naked House, Kawagoe, Saitama, Japan

Architect: Shigeru Ban Architects: Shigeru Ban, Anne Scheou, Mamiko Ishida, project team
Consultants: Hoshino, engineer
Contractor: Misawaya Kesetsu
Photography: Hiroyuki Hirai

De Blas House, Madrid, Spain

Architect: Estudio Arquitectura Campo Baeza: Alberto Campo Baeza, principal. Raul del Valle Gonzalez
Consultants: Concepcion Perez Gutierrez, structural engineer; Francisco Melchor, project management
Contractor: Juan Sainz
Photography: Hisao Suzuki

Sheep Farm House, Kyneton, Victoria, Australia

Architect: Denton Corker Marshall Pty Ltd.
Consultants: Bonacci Winward, engineers
Contractor: Multiplex Constructions
Photography: Tim Griffith

Flooded House, Istanbul, Turkey

Architect: GAD Architecture: Gokhan Avcioglu, principal in charge; Salih Kucuktuna, Durmus Dilekci, project team
Consultants: ENKA, engineers; Adepa & Hale Soyer, lighting
Contractor: ENKA
Photography: Ali Bekman

Peninsula House, Victoria, Australia

Architect: Sean Godsell Architect: Sean Godsell, principal; Hayley Franklin
Consultants: Sam Cox, landscape architect; Felicetti, structural engineer
Contractor: Kane Constructions
Photography: Earl Carter

Villa Eila, Mali, Guinea

Architect: Heikkinen-Komonen Architects: Mikko Heikkinen, Markku Komonen, partners in charge;
Simo Freese, project architect; Bjorn Julin, site manager; Souleyman Djallo, coordinator
Photography: Onerva Utriainen

Dyngby House, Jylland, Denmark

Architect: Claus Hermansen Architects MAA: Claus Hermansen, principal; Jonas Qvesel, project team
Contractor: Ivar Madsen
Photography: Poul Ib Hendriksen, Anders Kavin & Claus Hermnasen

Mirzan House, Kuala Lumpur, Malaysia

Architect: Kerry Hill Architects: Kerry Hill, Mark Ritchie, Chris Lee, Simon Cundy, project team
Consultants: GDP Architects, associate architects; Tieera Design, landscape designers; Frazer Worley,
structural engineer; Jurutera Perunding Vandun, mechanical and electrical engineers
Contractor: Builder Enterprise
Photography: Albert Lim

238

Dayton House, Minneapolis, Minnesota

Architect: Vincent James Architect & Associates: Vincent James, principal; Douglas Dank, Paul Yaggie,
Nancy Blankfard, Andrew Dull, Nathan Knutson, Steve Lazen, Robert Loken, Mark Noland, Taavi
Somer, Kate Wyberg, project team
Consultants: Hargreaves Associates, landscape architects; James Carpenter, glass; Powell/Kleinschmidt,
interior design; Carroll, Franck & Associates, engineers; Betker/Stangeland, structural engineers
Contractor: Yerigan Construction
Photography: Don Wong

House 75, Cantagua, Chile

Architect: Mathias Klotz Architect: Mathias Klotz, principal; Elodie Fulton, collaborator
Consultants: Enzo Valladares, engineer
Contractor: Moravia
Photography: Mathias Klotz

Laminata House, Leerdam, the Netherlands

Architect: Kruunenberg van der Erve Architects: Gerald Kruunenberg & Pal van der Erve, principals.
Consultants: St.Gobain-Glass-Netherlands, glass engineer; Van Rijn & Partners, structural engineer (except glass); Legrand Netherlands bv,electronical; W/E Consultants Sustainable Building; the Netherlands Organization for applied Scientific Research (TNO) Department Industry and department Building, pre-design
Contractor: St.Gobain-Glass-Netherlands
Photography: Christian Richters, Luuk Kramer

Kundoo House, Auroville, India

Architect: Anupama Kundoo Architect
Photography: Andreas Deffner

Unfolding House, Bangkok, Thailand

Architect: LOOM Studio: Raveevarn Choksombatchai & Ralph Kirk Nelson, principals.
Consultants: Methee Rusamee, Local Architect; Jedsada Pritanan, Structural Engineer
Photography: Wison Thuraweerasuk, Ralph Kirk Nelson

Kangaroo Valley House, Kangaroo Valley, New South Wales, Australia

Architect: Glenn Murcutt, principal; Nick Sissons, assistant.
Contractor: Jim Anderson/Boardwalk
Photography: Anthony Browell

Eco-Aluminum House, Tsukuba, Ibaraki, Japan

Architect: Kazuhiko Namba + KAI Workshop: Kazuhiko Namba, principal.
Consultants: Ijima Architect Office, structural engineer
Contractor: Nikkei Sangyo
Photography: Hiro Sakaguchi, Kazuhiko Namba

Light House, Seattle, Washington, USA

Architect: Olson Sundberg Kundig Allen Architects: Tom Kundig, design principal; Robert Jakubik, Aaron Schmidt
Consultants: Monte Clark Engineering, structural engineering; Richard Haag, landscape architect; Affiliated Engineers, mechanical/electrical engineering; Janice Viekman, interior design; Gulassa & Company, Eisenwerk, Jim Rizotto, DogPaw and Empire Welding.
Contractor: Charter Construction
Photography: Paul Warchol Photography

Vancouver House, Vancouver, British Columbia, Canada

Architect: Patkau Architects: Michael Cunningham, John Patkau, Patricia Patkau, Peter Suter, project team
Consultants: Fast and Epp Partners, engineers
Contractor: Glover Corporation
Photography: Paul Warchol Photography

Karjat Farmhouse, Karjat, Bombay, India

Architect: Samira Rathod Design Associates
Contractor: Asuram Mistry
Photography: Rajeshwar Mande

Cheval Place, London, England

Architect: Seth Stein Architect & Associates
Consultants: Alan Doorman, structural engineer; Double Parking Ltd, elevator engineer
Contractor: Underpin & Makegood Ltd
Photography: Richard Bryant / Arcaid

Tree House, Cape Town, South Africa

Architect: van der Merwe Miszewski Architects
Consultants: Tama Kiitzner, landscape architect; Henry Fagan & Partners, structural engineer; Bernard James & Partners, surveyors
Contractor: Scalabrino Construction
Photography:Steven Inngs, Ronnie Leveton, van der Merve Mizsowski Architects

240

Studio House, Beijing, China

Architect: Ai Wei Wei
Photography: Ma Xiaochun

Stone Cloud House, Seoul, South Korea

Architect: Kyu Sung Woo Architect Inc.: Kyu Sung Woo, principal; Andrew Wang, Dong Hyeog Choi, Stephen Lacker, Joon Bahng, Sheryl Kurtz-Halberstadt, Marty McCammon, Austin Smith, Todd Thiel, Brian Mulder, project team.
Consultants: Dyne Architects-Consulting Engineers, associate architect; Berg Howland Associates, lighting.
Contractor: Shin Han Construction
Photography:Timothy Hursley